Individualized Instruction

A Book of Readings

Individualized Instruction

A Book of Readings

E. GENE TALBERT
Arizona State University

LARRY E. FRASE
Arizona State University

CHARLES E. MERRILL PUBLISHING COMPANY
A Bell & Howell Company
Columbus, Ohio

Published by
Charles E. Merrill Publishing Co.
A Bell & Howell Company
Columbus, Ohio 43216

International Standard Book Number: 0-675-09096-2

Library of Congress Catalog Card Number: 77-189326

1 2 3 4 5 6 7 8 9 10/76 75 74 73 72

Printed in the United States of America

Preface

Continuous progress for each child is increasingly the central goal of school systems. The most promising practice for realizing it appears, at this time, to be individualized instructional programs. Within such programs, each pupil can proceed in an appropriate direction at his own pace without the drawbacks inherent in traditional grouping procedures. Transition to such a program, however, is not easy. Teacher preparation has been geared to instruction of groups with the teacher playing the leadership role. Individualized instruction requires dramatically different procedures and roles. Teachers want to make these changes and are asking for information which will facilitate them.

Individualized instruction within a public school setting is in an infant state. Many unsettled issues remain. We do not believe that all the perfect answers can now be laid out for all to follow. In recent years, however, numerous articles have appeared which suggest possible directions. From these and other current sources, we have attempted to compile material which gives a sound basis for individualized instruction, identifies important components of it, and points out some of its expected outcomes. They have been chosen with the teacher who has questions in mind, and, we believe, they will help teachers in choosing and facilitating changes they want to make.

We are deeply grateful to teachers with whom we've worked in workshops for the questions they've raised which have guided our choice of material. Obviously, the contents of this book come from many writers and publications. Their permission to use this material is greatly appreciated.

E. Gene Talbert
Larry E. Frase

Contents

Individualized Instruction

A Book of Readings

I

Individualized Instruction: Why Individualize?

The enormous magnitude of individual differences among members of a class group and even within a given individual are well known to everyone who has worked with children. Such easily observed traits as height, weight, and manual dexterity make this obvious. Examination of intelligence and achievement test scores reveal that differences are not limited to physical and motor characteristics. In a seventh grade class taught by one of the editors, intelligence quotients, as measured by a widely used test, ranged from 63 to 155. These data indicate a mental age range of more than ten years. It has been estimated that, at fourth grade and above, the number associated with the grade level is a conservative estimate of the achievement range in years. Thus, the seventh grade group above could be expected to have at least a seven year spread in achievement in any given area. A more exact estimate would probably exceed nine years. Many recent studies raise additional issues related to differences in learning styles and relative strengths of usable motives.

Our national ideals demand that every child should have an opportunity to realize his potential. Conformity to group standards is out of step with such a purpose. We are accountable to our society to strive for these ideals in the fullest measure possible. At the present time, the only feasible means of approaching this goal is individualized instruction.

The first group of articles has been selected to show the relationship between our cognitive and affective ideals and individualized instruction, give some general procedures which facilitate individualized instruction, provide motivation for initiating individualized instruction, and give a limited view of what individualized instruction really is.

John I. Goodlad

Toward 2000 A.D. in Education

There was more intensive activity in education during the decade that began in 1957 than there was at any other period in the history of this country.

What legacy has this activity left us?

From the educational standpoint, I suppose the most significant thing that happened during this decade was the curriculum reform movement. It more than anything else, has left us with a way of dealing with knowledge.

The curriculum reform movement says to us: Look, you cannot teach all the old facts; perhaps you should not pay very much attention to any facts except for instrumental purposes. These instrumental purposes are intended to draw youngsters' attention to the fact that underlying man's organized knowledge are basic concepts and principles which sustain themselves for periods of 10, 30, and sometimes 50 years. If we can help youngsters grasp the idea that this is what knowledge is all about, then they may be able to cope with knowledge.

As part of the legacy of the "education decade," we have a new faith in the ability of children to learn solid fare by themselves. In

---

John I. Goodlad, "Toward 2000 A.D. in Education," *NCEA Bulletin* 65 (August 1968): 16-22.

Reprinted from the August 1968 issue of the *NCEA Bulletin* journal of the National Catholic Educational Association, Suite 350, One Dupont Circle, N.W., Washington, D.C. 20036.

Bruner's *The Process of Education*, we have the dictum that any kind of respectable materials can be learned in some sort of respectable way by any child at any age. This is an oversimplification, but it has been a very powerful factor in the current curriculum movement.

Another factor has been the production of materials that youngsters may use directly without the intervention of the teacher. Incidentally, I think it's an insult to teachers to say that they must not see such material — that it must go directly to the youngsters.

A third notion in the legacy from the education decade has been the enormous interest in individual differences in students and in efforts to deal with these differences.

I am sure that last year there were hundreds — perhaps thousands of conferences, institutes and workshops on individual differences. Yet, according to Patrick Suppe's work on computer-assisted instruction at Stanford University, we probably know more about individual differences and do less about them than we do in any other area of schooling.

As part of this large interest in individualized instruction, we have had a very deep interest in nongraded schools. It is very difficult for me to realize that it is nine years since our book on nongrading came out. Yet I discover that the interest in the theme is greater now than it was then.

In 1955 I was able to identify only 16 schools in the United States that called themselves nongraded. Now there are thousands that call themselves nongraded. My emphasis on the word "call" is deliberate.

We have also developed a great interest in team teaching — this idea is a very powerful one because it offers an opportunity to shake down the entire school in regard to how youngsters are grouped and the way resources are used. It offers potential for opening the schools to specialists of various kinds, to groupings of various sizes. But unfortunately, most of our team-teaching techniques are a long way from being the kinds of models some persons have set up theoretically.

Then, of course, we have modular scheduling. With the school day broken down into 20-minute periods, a youngster is able to put together any combination of such periods.

And there is great concern for the disadvantaged. Various kinds of supplementary programs—Upward Bound, Head Start, and other education programs — are designed to provide a better opportunity for disadvantaged youngsters.

I think, however, that in many of our efforts to deal with individual differences, we pay little attention to the single human being in the learning setting.

We have been much concerned about this because of young people's rejection of the kind of society many of us have espoused. They seek, in some instances, something more profound. I have been struck by the fact that in so many of our proposals for dealing with alienation at the college level, for example, we are still *unwilling* to give to the student any authority, any responsibility, any role in planning.

I have mentioned some aspects of our legacy from the "education decade." It is heady stuff. But, sometimes as I fly back and forth across the United States, so that I can be an expert on the East Coast where I cannot be one on the West Coast, I look about me with that airy, ethereal feeling, of flying over the clouds, and as I see those great rolling cumulonimbus clouds down below, I sometimes wonder if only they are filled with educational reform. I sometimes wonder how much water those clouds are dropping on the thirsty fields below. And, on the basis of my participation in symposia and conferences throughout the country, I think there is one group of people who talk about the brave new world in education and another group of people who have had very little opportunity to catch a glimpse of this world — much less to understand what it means.

So I would like to summarize what I believe to be the state of schooling in 1968. And I believe that what I shall say is as relevant for the Catholic schools of this nation as it is for the public schools.

My thoughts are based upon a series of studies in which I have been involved, including a nationwide study in 1961-2 of the education of American teachers.

Curriculum Reform

Clearly, there are shortcomings in the current curriculum reform movement. Rather than getting at the notion that knowledge is what one perceives at any given time, instead we are teaching a highly systematized, supposedly sequential body of material. And to step aside from that material is very difficult. There are few second chances, because we assume that the curriculum is cumulative. Yet we are getting evidence which suggests that the curriculum is far from cumulative; that the placement of subject matter, *even in curiculum reform*, is a highly arbitrary kind of thing; and that the kinds of sequences we have been talking about may not exist.

For example, Joseph Lipson at the University of Pittsburgh discovered that when he taught 11- and 12-year olds the very same physics concepts which were taught to freshmen at the University of Pittsburgh, the 11-and 12-year olds did almost as well as the freshmen.

We are beginning to see that our search for a very careful and systematic ordering of subject matter may indeed be quite arbitrary and that youngsters learn what they are taught.

I am growing increasingly concerned also that in the curriculum reform movement there is virtually no discussion of ends. What is this material supposed to produce? What kind of human beings? What kinds of thinking?

The instruments used to determine how well we are doing are almost entirely on the cognitive level — at the lowest levels at that.

We are talking about producing teachers, and we have led ourselves to believe that if youngsters are a mass of information about education they will be able to teach.

And when one raises questions about the behavior of human beings in our society and attempts to draw some links between this and their performances in school, the comparisons are indeed discouraging. We have been dealing in the past decade with the question: What can children learn at an early age? It is about time we returned to first principles and asked ourselves: What should youngsters learn at an early age? What knowledge is of most worth? But, even more fundamental: What kind of human beings are we trying to produce?

It has become clear that the curriculum — no matter how scientific, no matter how carefully arranged — is not gripping a significant part of our youngsters. I get the feeling sometimes that, at the junior high school in particular, much of what youngsters do in school constitutes an unwelcome intrusion on their daily lives.

The Classroom

We have brought up a generation of teachers on deductive thinking, telling and questioning. Our observations in the classroom showed us very clearly that the predominant teaching techniques today do not pertain to children learning for themselves but to questions and answers. It's teacher-to-child, child-to-teacher, teacher-to-child,

child-to-teacher, with very little cross discussion, small group activity, and so forth. Our data brings this out overwhelmingly at all levels of education, although least of all at the kindergarten level.

A couple of years ago I spent a day or two looking at curriculum reform projects. Then I visited the schools that were using the materials on an experimental basis, assuming that I would see the best things put into practice.

I remember spending two and a half days getting immersed in a project on inductive thinking, and then I visited nearby schools. The first visit was scheduled for 10:20. I arrived at 10:15. As I was entering the classroom I almost tripped over a cluster of youngsters gathered around a turtle. When the teacher saw me, she said: "Children put away the turtle, we are going to have science."

So we had crabs — because crabs happened to be the topic scheduled in this particular science program.

You see what I am getting at? We are still tied up in our deductive processes and have not arrived at the inductive ones.

That same day I walked into another classroom. The teacher was saying: "Children, we are talking these days about a new kind of procedure in education and it is called induction. The seven principles of induction are . . ."

Telling and questioning, limited small group work, and precious little provision for individual differences were evident even in a program which was supposed to be geared to the individual learning rates of youngsters. We have a long way to go. Clearly, textbooks still constitute the basic medium of instruction. This was supported by a study of principles by the NEA in 1962 and reconfirmed by our own studies.

The general impression I have received in many instances is that we have walled-off classrooms in walled-off schools.

I was particularly struck by this aspect while visiting American schools abroad about a year and a half ago. I visited many essentially private schools run by local communities for American children, and for many other children in the community. In some instances the schools were supported in part by the U.S. Department of State.

Here are some of the questions I asked in these schools: Do you ever have people coming in with the music of Iran? Do you ever have writers and poets coming into the classroom? Do you ever take the youngsters out to look at Singapore Harbor? Do the children ever get on some of those wonderful boats in the harbor?

The answer to each question was "No."

When I asked why, the answer I got (which I refuse to accept) is that all of these parents felt they were abroad for a temporary period and that their children had to "fit in" when they returned to Palo Alto, or Davenport — or you name it.

Here were children sitting in the richest of cultures, at a wonderfully impressionistic time of their lives, but they were exposed to a locked-in curriculum. We are only playing games if we regard it as sequential. We are only playing games if we think that youngsters who do not return to that "unit" in southern California will be any worse off with respect to the good life and the good society.

As for our instructional approach to education, it's preschool; then elementary in preparation for secondary education; secondary is the gateway to higher education; and higher education contributes to the gross national product.

Have we ever thought of education for education's sake. And education's sake means for the individual's sake.

Little Innovation

In our tours across the United States, we found little sign of honest-to-goodness organizational innovation. I have been pushing organizational innovation for a long time, not because I think team teaching in and of itself changes curriculum and instruction; and not because I think that raising the ceilings and lowering the floor of a school is going to develop pupil readiness and is going to change the curriculum by itself. But you cannot live for long in a nongraded school with graded subject matter. And you cannot live for long in a truly nongraded school with graded textbooks.

The purpose of a nongraded school is not to disguise individual differences by grouping youngsters in little compartments, but to expose the individual differences. When I see people locked into their little levels plan and their little groups, which they pretend are homogenous, I realize that the concept of nongrading has hardly begun.

We did not find nongraded schools on our tour. We did not find much team teaching. Computer-assisted instruction barely exists, except in a few experimental centers. I maintain that individually prescribed instruction will not have swept the country by 1971, as some articles have said.

For a considerable period of time the computer will be used to handle masses of data — personnel information, salaries, budgets —

but computer-assisted instruction is some distance away. I would say that computer-assisted instruction in our schools will become a functioning reality in a good many communities across the United States and be taken seriously as part of the teaching team sometime after 1980.

We are beginning to realize that the school as it usually exists now is not a very intense learning environment.

We have thought that if we improved the curriculum and instruction, we would take care of 80% or 90% of the ball game. We may be taking care of only 20% or 30% of the ball game. Or even if it is 50% or 60%, there is an enormous proportion of what a youngster learns outside of the school environment.

Our real problem is how do we increase the intensity of the school? How do we provide opportunity for divergence and creativity, and for behavior which runs counter in many instances to our ideas of what it should be?

Education Tomorrow

In regard to education tomorrow, I have suggested elsewhere that probably we are already in three overlapping phases of schooling. We have been in the first phase since schools began. I like to call this human-based schooling, that is, we have had schools run for humans by humans. We have not introduced much in the way of machines. Motion pictures and filmstrips have not really caught on. We saw very few used during our trips. Yet there are so many marvelous educational films and filmstrips available to us today!

Lately we have had a great intensification of human-based schooling. Individualized instruction, nongrading, team teaching — all of these things are designed to help human beings work with human beings. And yet, in spite of this, we do not have a school that is the intensely human environment we would like it to be. So I predict that for about the next 15 years we will be preoccupied with attempting to make the schools we have, with the ideas we now have, more intensely human. I do not think we need tack on many more human innovations. I do not think any innovation is powerful enough to change the school the way it needs to be changed. Instead we need to examine the means of schooling, using some of the greatest guiding ideas about the aims of schooling.

Already we see another kind of school on the horizon, a school in which human beings and machines are going to have to learn to work side-by-side. Computers will not guide a large percentage of learning by 1970, but they will guide a great deal of it by 1990.

It is now economically possible to put a computer terminal in every elementary classroom in the United States for a cost of one five-hundredth of what we will spend on elementary education in the next decade. That is not an exorbitant cost.

We as teachers will try in the classroom to intervene between the computer and the child. We will be lost if we try to determine during the day when to plug in with the computer. The moment that human beings start monitoring computers, they will be in trouble. They can't keep up.

One of the things that disturbs me as I look at computer-assisted instruction is the number of human beings it takes to keep the children on the computers.

I think that we will have to assign to the computer the lesser human learnings, such as the beginnings of literacy, even the basic concepts of mathematics, and a great deal of routine work having to do with the structure of language and spelling.

It is interesting to watch the computer at the University of Pittsburgh teaching a youngster to spell. The youngster sits there before a terminal that looks like a television set. The machine says: "Write necessary." The youngster writes with a stylus on the TV screen. If he makes a mistake it is removed and the machine says: "Look at the word." The youngster looks at the word "necessary." The computer says: Write the word. The youngster is supposed to write the word "necessary" under the word that appears in front of him. This time if he makes a mistake the computer gets angry.

In the course of time we will be able to assign the lower literacies to the computer, and we human teachers will be able to engage in the truly human things. What will the teacher do if the 70% to 80% of the routine tasks which probably could be computerized now are assigned directly to the computers and to terminals for the children and they, proceeding at their own rate, make fewer errors than they make now? Clearly, a fundamental restructuring of teacher education and rethinking of the role of the teacher is called for.

Therefore, what we need on an experimental basis is not just more research on how to sequence and program material for the computer, but studies of human beings and computers working side-by-side, so that we may develop taxonomies of who does what, how and when.

And this is going to take an intense kind of experimental work with human beings — work that most researchers are not equipped to undertake.

I propose that we establish across the country — perhaps in our Catholic schools, because they should have more freedom to experiment — a few centers in which we can begin to work with the new technology. However, our purpose will not be to program the machines, but to study how human beings and machines can work together productively.

I suspect that the interim step is to have human beings learn to work side-by-side without a machine.

I am told that each computer terminal put in an elementary school classroom today would cot $2,000. If we were to decide to install them now, I think the price of each computer terminal would drop to $1,000 in a very short time.

About the time that we move into the period of the 1980s and have more programs for the computer, private enterprise in this country is going to become increasingly aware that if you can put a computer terminal in every classroom why not put a computer terminal in every home? The moment we make that decision the cost of the computer terminal will go down to the price of a television set. This means that the third era of schooling involves a computer terminal in the home, plugged into whole variety of learning opportunities.

But if computers for educational purposes have not received the humanizing touch, the computer in the home will be no better than television in the home.

In viewing learning and teaching for the year 2000 and beyond, it is easier to predict what will not happen than what will.

There is no need for us to believe that there should be a schoolhouse. We must stop thinking about school as just a physical entity.

About three years ago a school superintendent in California said to me: "You know it's fine for you to have a laboratory school in a university, but what we really need is a laboratory school in a public school system. I am going to create one."

"When is it going to open?" I asked.

"In about 15 months," he said.

"How many are you going to hire?" I asked.

"Well," he said, "we have 600 children. Our ratio is 28 to 1. We will need about 22 teachers."

I said, "Why hire 22? Why not five?"

He looked at me in horror and said, "I have 600 children."

I said, "I know, but if you had only five teachers you could have more instructional material and other resources than any other school in America. That would make you unique."

He looked a bit perturbed.

"What size building are you going to have?" I asked.

"I need a building for 600 children," he said.

I said "Why don't you build a building for 300?"

"But I have 600 children," he said.

"I realize that," I said, "but if you build a building for 300, you can take the other one million dollars or whatever you have left and, along with the amortization, you will have more resources for taking these children out into the real world for part of their education. The climate in California is delightful; the children do not need to be locked up in a building all day. Half of the school children could be in the school building every day and the other half could be somewhere else."

By this time he was very upset. But the point is that if we rethink schooling from the beginning we might have only a few buildings; we might have different kinds of buildings; or we might just have guidance centers where youngsters start before they go out to explore the rest of the world.

We are proposing in a set of recommendations we are now making at the federal level that there be various kinds of clusterings around a community for youngsters who wish to engage in educational activities that the school does not provide.

In the year 2000 we will not have to have a prescribed age for beginning school. The computer console with an array of stimuli and feedback devices will be as natural for the child of the year 2000 as the computer is today.

Teaching and learning will not be marked by a standard day of from 9 a.m. to 3 p.m., a standard year of September until June, a specific year for a grade, or many of the other things we are accustomed to.

And there will not be any less learning because of no class periods, no Carnegie units, no ringing of bells, no jostling of pupils from class-to-class.

The student will be free to concentrate exclusively on a given field for weeks or months, or to divide his time among the available fields of interest, because human energy will not be the predominant factor in what, when and how a youngster learns.

The role of teachers will change markedly. Many teachers will spend little time in direct contact with children. A great deal of their time will be spent in preparing lessons which will be viewed and used by millions of people.

School as we know it will be replaced by a very diversified learning environment, which will involve the home, parks, museums, art centers, guidance centers, and other aspects of the environment.

It is quite conceivable that each community will have a learning center and that homes will contain an electric console connected to a central generating unit. With a touch of the finger you will have many cultural and learning activities available.

The most controversial issues of the 21st century will be the issues that face us today: What are goals of human behavior and the means of modifying it? And who shall determine these goals and means?

The first educational question will not be what knowledge is of most worth, but what kind of human beings do we wish to produce.

It seems to me, that as educational leaders we have to be concerned about becoming as well informed as we can about the new substances of education. We have to inform ourselves about new ways of instituting processes for change. We must work out strategies that are no longer accidental: not just speeches, not just symposia, but experimental schools where we are deliberately developing the new procedures so that teachers who indeed do "want" to know may observe and learn.

Are we going to get bogged down in trivia? Are we going to debate report cards? Are we going to debate whether a little bit of subject matter should come here or there? Are we going to play the game of coverage? Up to here by Halloween? Up to here by Christmas?

We must get down to truly fundamental questions. To what extent are young people coming into critical possession of their culture? To what extent is each individual being provided with opportunities to become his unique self? To what extent is each individual developing a deep sense of personal worth?

When the laboratory high school at Ohio State University was closed down a few years ago, a graduate of that institution said to me: "How sad! Do you know what that school did for me? It made me feel that I was somebody." I thought: What a tribute to a school!

As a citizen and as an educator, the question I think most important is: What kind of human beings do we wish to produce?

I conclude with a quotation made by President Johnson in 1965. I think it is as highly relevant today as it was then.

> *If we are learning anything from our experiences, we are learning that it is time for us to go to work. And the first work of these times and the first work of our society is education.*

Albert H. Shuster

Theory and Philosophy of the Emerging Elementary School

The American Society has changed vastly in this century in respect to population and technology, forms of power and social organization. The late President Kennedy once said: "Just as every apparent blessing contains the seeds of danger, every area of trouble gives out a ray of hope, and the one unchangeable certainty is that nothing is certain or unchangeable."

The noted historian, Arnold Toynbee, stated that many a powerful civilization perished because the people failed to adapt their ways to changing world conditions. In many respects, we in this country have been very forward and progressive; in other ways we have been reluctant to change, even when the change might have meant better things for our children.

Few people in the American society question the desirability of replacing the icebox with the electric refrigerator, the outdoor privy with indoor facilities, the horse and buggy with the modern, sleek automobile; and, as you know, there is an unlimited list of technological changes which each of us could further enumerate. Changes in education are also imminent, but even today far too

---

Speech delivered at the Conference on Early Primary Education at the University of Kansas, Lawrence, Kansas, September 30, 1967.

Albert H. Shuster, "Theory and Philosophy of the Emerging Elementary School," *The University of Kansas Bulletin of Education* 22 (Winter 1968): 37–45.

many schools are using outmoded, obsolete instructional programs which still demand that the learners memorize isolated bits of unrelated information.

The failure of education to meet successfully the challenges of change could very well spell the end of American democracy and freedom. This, in my opinion, is because education is the backbone of today's modern technological society. All groups, regardless of their social or economic place in life, must be in a position to actively participate in making decisions which affect them. I need not review for you here the many changes which have come across the world since we first started on our path to independence on the "battlegreen" of Lexington. The forces of increased population, of science and technology, of social and economic change, and satisfactions of wants and desires would not let America stand still.

Some Aspects of the Education Reform Movement

American education is on the threshold of a great revolution which will result in a dynamic new approach to mass education. I regret that I am not far-seeing enough to draw a picture for you with all the details of the school of the future. But I do know that nongraded schools are, and will continue to be, a component of this educational reform.

The explosion of knowledge has resulted in more difficult curriculum decisions. Subject specialists have been brought into education through the federal government, through large foundations, and through various professional associations. We have now available from psychologists, sociologists, and anthropologists more valid information about people and how they learn. Bruner, in his provocative book titled *The Process of Education*, states that "any subject can be taught effectively in some intellectually honest form to any child at any stage of development."[1] This is a bold hypothesis but an essential one in thinking about the nature of curriculum. I know of no evidence to contradict it, but there is much evidence to support it.

We are beginning to look at the professionalization of teaching and teaching-related roles. This is a part of this revolution. We are only scratching the surface in this area. Team teaching is the beginning of an organizational plan which is helping teachers to redefine their roles and to recognize their strengths and weaknesses. No teacher can do the whole job equally as well as a team which is capitalizing on each member's particular strength. We are now aware of the value of para-professionals and are learning how to use them, but we have much to do in changing our attitudes about such aides. Some teachers are still saying "I'd rather not have them around. I don't want to be bothered with someone else in the classroom." On the other hand, a project with which I've been associated has been training high school students to serve as teacher aides. Feedback from this project strongly indicates that teacher attitudes about the usefulness of teacher aides can and will change. Such remarks as "I don't know how I've gotten along all these years without them," and "they are so helpful — I have more time now to devote to certain children who need more help" are indications of change in attitude and appreciation for teacher aides by veteran teachers.

The final point I wish to make at this time relating to the background of the reform movement is that we have given lip service for many decades to the theory of individualization of instruction, but we have built up "straw men" or we have been fighting shadows which have kept us from really getting at the heart of the problem. One of our national goals is to strive toward excellence; however, we have not accepted this goal for all. Each person must be in a program which provides for excellence in helping him to fulfill his own potential. This is to say that excellence is not only for the gifted child, but for *all* children. When we recognize that our task is to promote diversity in the process of growth, we then will be aware of the uniqueness of each child. This means that our achievement scores should become more widely dispersed rather than closer together. But, to the contrary, we have established a rigid, monolithic, one-dimensional program which is inappropriate for more than half of our pupils. We have today a growing rejection of an idea of education as having a fixed beginning or end point set out into neat little packages called grade levels. However, educational progress has come to be recognized as continuous and endless with an emphasis upon continuity in learning related only to the individual's readiness and maturity for the content at hand. Thus the task is helping children to learn how to learn.

The Challenge of Nongradedness

No term seems to adequately define what we call the nongraded school. I have known of large numbers of parents who were under the impression that this term simply meant a school where no grades or report cards were given out. For the purpose of this discussion, then, let us say that a nongraded school is one in which teachers try to make truly suitable provisions for the individual differences found in children. In such a school there is a recognition of the context within which youngsters learn. Thus the school organization might be defined as being developmental in nature with no clearly defined levels separating any one group from another. Goodlad has stated that "many schools in the United States carry the nongraded label. But none has fully achieved what is envisioned for nongradation . . . this gulf is largely due to the need for reform in all those factors on which nongrading depends." He further states that "because of a misunderstanding of the true meaning of nongradedness, many schools have fallen into a pitfall equally as bad as the graded school by over-organizing groups into levels."[2]

Now what nongrading refers to is more than just eliminating grade level lines and the grade level structure of the school program, but replacing it with a plan which has been called continuous progress. In this plan the learners advance at whatever rates they are capable of mastering the learning materials in the curriculum areas.

The new school must have a definable commitment to serving the individual. Such a school will have teachers who try to make suitable provisions for individual differences. This will require that the teachers be specialists in the psychology of learning and possess an understanding of child development. In addition, they will need to know the content of the skill subjects to be mastered since such a program requires that the content in the curricular areas be set up in continuous sequence. To make suitable provisions for each successive educational experience for each child is essential to provide for the child's needs at the appropriate moment of his development. Children who are learning at their own level of maturity will need to be programmed into each curriculum area. Thus the learner will be involved in such activities as independent study, tutorial learning, product producing, discussion or decision-making, and finally activities which involve viewing, listening, and receiving of information. Nonc of these activities in a nongraded school are thought to be used to the exclusion of the other, but their use will be related to the learner's particular need at the time. These are the components of the context in which instruction emerges and pupils learn. In these situations the pupils will have the opportunity to interact with teachers or other pupils. In such a situation the learner is interacting with someone who serves as an agent of something he needs, such as knowledge, skills, or attitudes to be developed. If his learning requires certain resources, then the interaction is between the individual and the resources or materials such as tape or film.

The general purpose of the nongraded school then would be to make better provision for individual differences among learners. These differences manifest themselves among groups of children who are at the same chronological age. There are differences in maturity, differences in physical growth, differences in rate of learning. Since these differences all affect the rate of learning to a considerable extent, the pupil's rate of learning then depends on the experiences he has had at any given time in his life. These differences do not necessarily depend on native ability, as I am sure we all know. Recent research on intelligence test scores show conclusively that an I.Q. score, which is a measure of performance, is affected at least equally by the learning experiences which the individual has had as it is by the particular level of native capacities that he happened to possess at birth. We are all aware of the fact that within any given individual there are differences in maturity and learning rate from one curriculum area to another. Thus nongrading needs to provide for *intra*-individual differences, as well as inter-individual differences. The basic reason, then, underlying the development of nongrading as an organizational approach as well as a philosophical approach to instruction has to do with the increasing recognition of individual differences and the recognition, also, of the difficulties standing in the way of taking account of these differences within the usual grade system.

Individualizing Learning

The educational program in the nongraded school must be one in which teachers try to make truly suitable provisions for the fact of individual differences. These arrangements depend upon how the teachers envision the educational program. That is, the successive educational experiences of each child will be essentially pertinent and appropriate to his needs at that moment of his development. The teacher needs to understand that logical order or sequence does not necessarily mean the way a given subject is presented in the textbook. Science, for example, has been presented traditionally in ten or more topics per grade. Now the approach is moving toward five areas of study which permit cycling back into an area one or more times after the initial approach. This provides for maturation of learners and permits them through the discovery approach to deal with an area of learning until they exhaust their capacities for comprehension at that level of their development; after further growth, they can be recycled into the same area of study to deal with the topic in greater depth. Children do not always learn according to some preconceived adult plan. Children studying energy may be inquisitive about a crane lifting steel to the top of a building. Although this would not be the logical place to begin the discussion of energy with 6- or 7-year-olds, it would be the opportune time to capitalize on interest. Some children might readily make the transition back to simple machines which do work for us to the more complex crane. (One 6-year-old girl I know recognized that energy for driving a toy was created by putting the spring under pressure by winding it. She then was able to generalize that it was from energy in food consumed by humans and other animals that they were able to do work.) The point is that certain children will be able to generalize about energy sooner than others; thus some children will need to be cycled back into the study of energy at another time, after they have had additional experiences and have grown more mature. The learning experience then should be so regulated that each child will be under just the right amount of pressure to encourage him to learn. This means that the below-average child should not be under the kind of pressure with which he was faced in the graded school, but perhaps the above-average child should be faced with a little more pressure than he met with in the graded school, the difference being that in the nongraded school we can redeploy youngsters for different kinds of individual and small group experiences to suit their particular needs.

When the pressure for learning is just right and the learning experience is the natural outgrowth of a strong motivation, success in the task to be achieved is more or less assured. Obviously, the pupil must be reasonably diligent, but this is virtually assured when the pressure for achieving is just right. Under such circumstances the curiosity to learn, which the child had when he entered kindergarten, is not lost but is enhanced. Far too many youngsters attend school every day without meeting one degree of success. Most of us would have given up long ago if we didn't achieve what I like to call an imbalance of praise over blame or failure. We all have known many days when we have asked ourselves, "What in the world did I accomplish today?" — days when the children were particularly restless, the paints were spilled, etc. If every day were like that we would soon give up completely. But then a particularly good day comes along and revives our enthusiasm once again. Certainly children need this same encouragement which comes from achieving some degree of success. The imbalance of praise over blame assures some recognition of tasks which have been performed satisfactorily and which lead to motivating the individual to continue his pursuit. On the other hand, psychological research supports, without a doubt, that continuous failure leads only to frustration and eventually to a lack of aspiration to even try to learn. Increased confidence in himself as a person and as a learner results when the child successfully achieves a task.

The nongraded school is void of grade labels such as first, second, third, etc.; in addition, there is an absence of all related policies of promotion and failure. But the inherent danger is in eliminating the traditional grades and establishing in their place twelve to sixteen different levels. We must look at children as individuals and not as fitting some scheme which causes each to be doing the same thing at the same time. Now what I'm saying is that teachers need to change their concepts of teaching. They need to recognize that learning is an individual matter and that children learn in their own way. If children are reading in a reading circle, for example, why must they all read from the same story in the same book? Is it not conceivable that they might each bring their own story to the circle and read the entire story to the group? Much will depend, of course, upon how the teacher views his or her role in this type of classroom.

A reporting system which indicates whether a child is living up to his potential needs to be developed in behavioristic terms and such a system needs to be based upon a continuous pupil evaluation program. If team teaching is the form of school organization operating in a nongraded philosophically oriented setting, then determining pupil potential is a team task. That is, the child's potential is not only determined by use of a variety of objective instruments, but also by his performance as observed by the team. Collective intelligence of the team is then utilized in arriving at a reasonably accurate estimate of the child's potential. When such a system is implemented in our schools, we will have made progress toward eliminating the constant injury which our evaluation and reporting systems are doing to children.

Team Teaching and the Nongraded School

I should like to point out that I believe that the success of the nongraded school is probably closely linked to team teaching. In fact, I believe that it is best to commit the school to team teaching before launching a nongraded program. Team teaching is a cooperative endeavor in which the strengths of each teacher are shared with the children through a flexible organization which permits teachers to share in planning, teaching, and appraising the learning situation. In this kind of a school organization, curriculum development is a continuous on-going process as teachers work together to meet the specific needs of children through the team effort. Provisions can be made to update curriculum content by assigning a team member to keep abreast of research and materials in one curriculum area. Such a teacher would then share his information with the team. The new technology must be linked with curricula and teaching methods to school organization. A child reacting to a specially prepared tape and recording this reaction for group consideration at a later date is an illustration of relating technology to curriculum.

Mastery in Learning

In our enthusiasm to use all of the new educational "hardware," we must exercise some caution to see that children do not become merely vessels for mechanical learning nor receptacles for teachers' ideas; instead, they should become self-determining learners. Instruction should be such that each child is taught so that mastery is achieved by each learner, but at his own pace. Perhaps the word "mastery" as used here, could be somewhat frightening because people tend to think of it as meaning complete and total knowledge or command of any given bit of knowledge or competency. Mastery implies a measure of retention in the learning act which enables the learner to use what he has learned as a stepping stone to other units of work in the same curriculum area. It further implies that the student will be able to use what he has learned with judgment and discrimination in situations appropriate to using the knowledge.

For some reason we seem to have lost sight of the concept of mastery and I believe this is one of the bases for looking at the nongraded school. We must accept the fact that *every* pupil has the right to learn well what he studies and *can* learn well what he studies if instruction is properly organized for each learner. In my judgment, the success of the nongraded school, as well as the success of the whole educational reform movement, depends upon our providing the type of organizational structure and approaches to instruction which will result in mastery for all students. The vast amount of "sloughing off" which we permit certain students to do is unjustified if we recognize that mastery can be accomplished if we are willing to create the type of instructional organization which permits each child to work at his own pace.

Using Programmed Learning

Programmed learning can make a major contribution to individualizing instruction. It does provide for letting students progress at their own rates. Now I would like to point out that many new programs are appearing in the market place and some of these are much improved over the earlier ones, but I believe the real danger in programmed instruction is that learning of tool subjects might be accomplished in the same mechanized way that traditional rote learning was. We need to recognize this inherent danger and see that students have small group experiences in critically examining their learning. Socialization of learning should come through small group discussions where children will learn not only to generalize from their learnings, but to acquire and employ the skills of critical thinking as well. Teachers will need to develop competencies in working with small groups so as to foster the development of those skills essential to democratic living. The common mistake is in using the same skills in small groups that we use in large groups. We need to develop questioning techniques which cause youngsters to compare and contrast if we are to develop critical thinking. There is no excuse for one-word answers and direct teacher-pupil recitation in a small group. Thus the effectiveness of the nongraded school is going to depend to a large degree upon the changes teachers can make in developing a repertoire of new skills and techniques.

A New Look at Curriculum

While the usual tool skills are important, other tools which we have neglected are also needed. Children can learn the skills necessary for effective decision making through an instructional process which places an emphasis on inquiry. Although each discipline has its own modes of inquiry, such as the scientist who uses the controlled experiment or the painter who combines elements of visual art into unique forms of expression, some specific techniques of inquiry are utilized by several disciplines. Such modes may be characterized by the nature and sources of the data, techniques of data collecting, processing, and recording, and the instruments and conceptual models used. In elementary school subjects such as art, each child must experience acting like an artist. That is, the child develops his skills by practicing in exploring art elements. He develops and refines his standards based on principles of good design. In far too many other areas of the curriculum the child is not given the opportunity to collect, process, and interpret data to the extent that he is permitted to reach his own conclusions. In most cases he is given facts and information and he is either told or reads the conclusions. Now, my point here is that the curriculum of the nongraded school should be more theoretical than information-giving. The curriculum should encourage children to practice thinking skills and involve them in inquiry activities which will foster independence in learning. In addition, the curriculum must provide (1) a greater emphasis at all instructional levels on the creative-expressive arts; (2) a more significant place in the child's day for health and physical development related to life-long recreational activities; and (3) increased emphasis on the problem-centered approach to science and social studies. The curriculum should also be divided into those items which can conveniently be set out in step sequence with mastery tests at each level. Other curriculum materials, independent of sequence, which lend themselves to special treatment then are separated from those which are necessarily ordered.

The one real handicap to the nongraded school is the task of completely individualizing instruction. However, this is about to be overcome through the use of computer-assisted instruction. CAI, as it is called, is now functioning quite effectively in a number of schools across the country. Although it is still in the experimental stages of development, it has been used successfully. A particularly interesting project is underway at Brentwood Elementary School located in Ravenswood School District, Palo Alto, California which has a portable classroom building equipped for computer assisted instruction. This system is both audio and visual. The audio may have up to two hours of message synchronized with the program. It is possible in this system to have the student's voice recorded back onto the audio track, using as much as forty minutes. The student's voice can then be played back and would be useful in working in reading, phonics, foreign language, or any type of learning which requires the student to interact with the visual or audio instruction. The system is currently being successfully used for reading and mathematics tutoring with heterogeneous elementary children.

This kind of instruction assistance might well help to reduce the teacher shortages. Under present school organizational designs there appears to be no way of securing enough teachers to really meet this shortage. Computer assisted instruction will call for master teachers and technicians who will work with the teachers as aides. We must, however, keep in mind that technology will not solve all of our problems. The role of the teacher will continue to be that of a diagnostician and determiner of appropriate learning experiences for each child.

Some Components of the Nongraded School

Now, in summary, let me reiterate the essential ingredients of a truly nongraded school:

1. Suitable provision is being made, in all aspects of the curriculum, for each unique child.
   a. This implies an adaptable, flexible curriculum.
   b. This implies flexible grouping and subgrouping.
   c. This implies a great range of materials coupled with new instructional technology.
2. The successive learning experiences of each child will be appropriate to his needs at that moment. This really is the creed which guides our professional decisions.
3. Each child is under just the right amount of pressure.
4. Success with appropriate rewards is assured for all kinds of learners so long as they do their tasks with responsible diligence and effort.
5. Grade labels and the related mechanisms of promotion and failure are not in evidence.
6. The reporting system is consistent with the philosophy that recognizes the uniqueness of each child.
7. There is a more sophisticated curriculum planning, evaluation, and record-keeping.

8. Provision is made for heterogeneous, multi-aged class groups. This implies that a nongraded class of children spanning several years would be preferable to a class or team of youngsters all about the same age.

In conclusion, I would like to state that we have only scratched the surface in studying and learning to deal with individual differences. In fact, we have only studied the end products of learning by our use of intelligence tests, aptitude tests, and achievement tests. I leave you with this thought which I believe we should answer if we are to reach our goal of nongraded or developmental schools for our children: "How do people differ as a result of the processes which affect behavioral change?" Once we can answer this question, the road ahead will be clear.

Notes

1. Jerome S. Bruner. *The Process of Education.* Harvard University Press, Cambridge, Mass. 1961. p. 33.

2. John I. Goodlad, John F. O'Toole, and Louise L. Tyler. *Computers and Information Systems in Education.* Harcourt, Brace & World, New York, 1966. p. 17.

Larry E. Frase

OPEN SPACE

Frequently, the term "open space" acts as a conjurer. Teachers envision a vast area of open space occupied by swarms of students abusing either each other or the furnishings and facilities which also occupy the "open space." Teachers and sometimes paraprofessionals also inhabit this pedagogically unwieldly environment. With this nightmare in full vision, the success of the open space concept, its applicability, and feasibility, to say the least, is on less than solid ground.

The preceding paragraph is surely exaggerated, but for some it approaches reality. To erase this nightmare, it can be said that open space does not necessarily imply classrooms or classes of students larger than those found in a conventional school. To be sure, open space *does not imply* a refinement of the following practices that characterize the traditional classroom: teachers involved in expository and didactic lecturing, students playing subordinate passive roles, stringent autocratic discipline and classroom procedures, and total concentration on cognitive learning. Open space *does imply* an "atmosphere" different from that generally found in classrooms. This new atmosphere is characterized by students making decisions (pertinent ones); selecting, at least partially, their own objectives; resolving conflicts; experiencing freedom to direct themselves; and most important, being responsible for their activities. It is important to say at this point that not all traditional pedagogy is bad for all students; it has served some well. At the same time, it is fundamental to indicate that the American culture has progressed and changed since its conception. Early in our history, education was needed to eliminate widespread illiterary; for the vast majority of citizens this objective has been accomplished. As the educative process grew in popularity, many more subjects were incorporated into the curriculum. As man's knowledge doubled and doubled again, the inability of the school to teach everything forced a fundamental shift to thinking skills and a renewed emphasis on learning desired attitudes. Part of the renewal emphasis on individualization is a response to this pressure.

Individualization is a practice that goes hand in hand with the open space concept. In fact, individualization is the vehicle or means through which the objectives of open space are realized. Therefore, open space can be considered as a plan for, or design of, individualization and can be represented in the form of the following model framework: objectives, knowledge, role of teacher, role of learner, organization, and evaluation. A closer examination of these elements may enhance understanding of the open space concept. (See Figure 1)

Elements of Open Space

Objectives The primary goal is to develop self-respecting, self-directing autonomous individuals.

The open space concept, a vehicle for individualization, is founded on the following premise: in an individualized program, children are expected to spend a considerable portion of their time working independently. *Independence* is the key word. Developing self-respecting, self-directing autonomous individuals results in a unique style of individualization — one that emphasizes independence. Independence implies freedom and freedom must imply responsibility; therefore, it is crucial that teachers see to it that students learn to handle their independence responsibly. "I have many freedoms, but I do not have the right to infringe on the rights of others." "I wonder what I should schedule for the 9:00 period? If I schedule math, I will miss the film, but if I schedule the film, I may not have my math assignment done for tomorrow." These statements are a sample of the types of concerns and expressions one might hear from children exploring the realm of the open space classroom and its accompanying rights and responsibilities. With this image in mind, school approaches life, not just an artificial preparation for it.

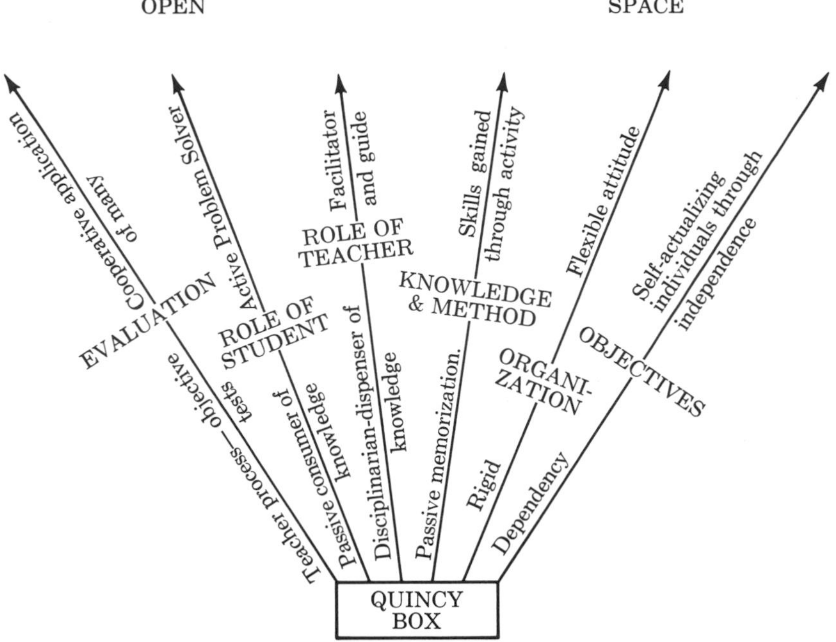

Figure 1. *A Model Framework for Open Space*

Knowledge and Method Cognitive or thinking processes are of primary importance; information is secondary.

In open space, subject matter is viewed as one vehicle which leads to sophisticated cognitive processes. Traditionally, many educators have been possessed with the idealistic tradition of teaching subject matter as though it were a composite of truisms enduring throughout eternity. Although it has been taught in good faith, the realization now is that subject matter facts are not enduring, but instead are temporary presumptions of truth. The temporary validity of facts has vast implications for the type of instructional processes to be used in our schools. The traditional method of instruction has been "expository" in nature. In an expository situation, the teacher communicates both the prerequisite knowledge and the advanced principles and conclusions to be dealt with. Although this method is still useful today, application of the following methods is encouraged with open space:

Guided Discovery The prerequisite knowledge or the principle and/or conclusion are communicated to the students by the instructor.

Directed Inquiry For each instructional objective the prerequisite information is communicated by the instructor in a hierarchical form. In this manner, concepts, principles, and solutions to problems are derived by the student as the result of verbal cues and prompts provided by the instructor.

In comparison, it can be seen that expository instruction stresses only content. The student is not provided any opportunities to make independent discoveries. In directed inquiry and guided discovery, both substansive knowledge and the methods for acquiring and utilizing knowledge are emphasized. Generally, but with some opposition, the following advantages for students are stated for directed inquiry and guided discovery:

1. Increased intrinsic motivation,
2. Development of a variety of inquiry approaches or response strategies that may be useful in a variety of learning situations.
3. Development of confidence and trust in the reliability of both the knowledge and inquiry skills.
4. Increased transfer and transfer efficiency.

Organization Nongraded or graded, team teaching or one teacher per classroom.

The open space classroom is not dependent on any organizational structure. Generally, nongradedness, team teaching, flexible scheduling, and computers come to mind when one thinks of open space and the schools that carry its label. This is truly a misinterpretation of the concept. One room, thirty-five students, conventional facilities, conventional instructional materials, plus one teacher with the desire and attitude to create open space are all that is needed for the implementation and maintenance of a successful open space classroom. The starting place for change is not organizational patterns, but discontent with the present roles of students in today's classrooms. A nongraded organization is possible; but at the same time an inflexible, autocratic classroom where little, if any, positive affective learning is occurring is also possible. Granted, nongraded vertical organization and team teaching can make a donation to open space, but their absence is certainly not a prohibiting factor to the teacher with desire to innovate and change the climate and procedures within the confines of his own classroom.

In the open space classroom, students are grouped on the basis of specific skill needs, common interests, or by tasks requiring diversified talents. The individual has choices. He may choose to work alone; he may wish to join a listening session; or he may choose to work with friends. At other times, the teacher may recognize the need to group students who demonstrate a need for instructional aid. Groups are temporary and constantly changing. They are formed with a goal in mind (cognitive or affective) and dissolved when the goal is accomplished.

Role of Student Includes decision-making, self-responsibility, self-direction and cooperativeness.

Traditionally, the American classroom has been characterized by an active role for the teacher and a passive and dependent role for the learner. A passive role for the learner has limited potentiality for affecting real learner change.

Open space provides an *active* role for the learner. Independent student behavior is the major goal of open space programs. There are several areas in which the student must play a much more active role. These include the following:

1. Decision-making
2. Self-responsibility
3. Self-direction
4. Cooperativeness

1. *Decision- or choice-making.* The following are examples of the types of decisions students may face when operating in an open space program:

a. After reading a behavioral objective, a student must decide whether he possesses the skill or knowledge indicated in the objective. If he feels he does possess the skills, he may attempt to pass the performance standard. He *may* attempt to do so. If he succeeds, he may by-pass that particular learning activity. If he does decide that he is deficient in the type of learning stated in the objective, he must carry out the learning activity.

b. When choosing a learning activity, the student must decide which learning activity he wants to do and which resources to utilize.

c. To prevent individualized programs from becoming a mechanical, lock-step process, a student should have freedom to demonstrate his accomplishment of the objective at any time during his learning activities. This calls for decision-making. Students will soon become skilled in determining when they are adequately prepared to pass a performance standard.

2. *Self-responsibility.* In any educational program, the student is ultimately responsible for his own learning. In contrast, students operating in an open space program are faced with more decisions than students operating in a conventional program, and, therefore, experience *more* responsibility than students operating in a traditional program. As previously mentioned, students operating in conventional programs experience too few situations involving self-direction, decision-making, and self-responsibility. Students operating in a successful individualized program have many opportunities to make choices and decisions, and, therefore, to develop responsibility. Although student self-responsibility is a necessity for the success of an open space classroom, it is not generally a behavioral characteristic of students beginning work in this type of program. Students must have the freedom and the opportunity to experience responsibility in order to develop a sense of self-responsibility. Therefore, it is important to keep in mind that students may misuse responsibility and make unfortunate decisions when confronted with their first experiences of this nature, but these mistakes are a vital element in the development of this characteristic.

3. *Self-direction.* As previously stated, students operating in an open space program do not receive the extensive direction from the teacher as do students in a more traditional setting. Students must begin to take the initiative to direct themselves and to ask themselves, "What do I do next?" And then *do* it. The following are

examples of situations where learners have the opportunity to ask themselves, "What do I do next?"

a. When deciding which resources to use.
b. When scheduling time.
c. Upon discovering that the resource chosen for use is not available.
d. Upon discovering that the film projector is not available or that the film is broken.
e. When unable to understand a learning activity.

These situations may be disconcerting to students who have never had opportunities to direct themselves, but through experience and with counseling concerning their experiences, a student can learn to direct himself. Here is an example of one situation a student might encounter.

> A student new to an open space classroom has just read his learning activity and proceeds to obtain appropriate materials. Problem! The materials cannot be found. The student does not know what to do, so his progress in the learning activity is halted. In this situation, the student may engage in activities disruptive to the group. At this time, punishment by the teacher is ill-advised. A discussion of alternative activities in this situation is suggested. Through this process, the student will become more efficient in managing similar situations in the future.

Of course, students should not be expected to direct themselves and/or know "what to do next" in every instance. In these situations, teachers should expect and encourage students to request help. "Teacher-help" systems are often effective. The following systems are suggested:

Flag system — students place a paper flag of specific color or shape on their desks.

Sign-up system — students sign-up on the chalkboard or "help list" when assistance is needed.

4. *Cooperativeness.* Cooperative behavior with teachers and fellow students is certainly a worthwhile objective. The type of cooperation referred to includes not only the informality of sharing re-

sources and being kind, which are important, but also a more formalized and educational form of cooperation, tutoring. This (tutoring) type of cooperation seldom occurs haphazardly. Teachers need to be familiar with each student's strengths and weaknesses so that pupils may be teamed according to their needs. Pairs can be formed where both members derive benefit from the association. Here is an example of tutoring in an open space classroom.

> John (age 11, grade 5) has been demonstrating behavior indicative of low self-concept. This behavior may be due to his poor achievement or vice-versa.
>
> Billy (age 8, grade 3) is having trouble learning to subtract.

With their permission, Billy and John could be teamed to work cooperatively on Billy's subtraction problem. Benefits for John may be two-fold.

1. Cognitive — Subtracting is easy for him so he gains a review and possibly a new understanding of the process.
2. Affective — Billy is John's new admirer. This enhances John's self-concept and his behavior.

Benefits to Billy are most likely to be derived only from the cognitive domain in the form of increased ability to subtract, but positive changes in affective behavior are possible. If Billy has no older brother and is in need of a "model" or "image" to respect and look up to, then John may fill this role.

Role of the teacher The teacher is a facilitator who acts as a guide and a resource person.

Often the teacher receives little attention in descriptions of the open space classroom. Because of this, it is often assumed that the teacher is actually of little importance. Nothing could be further from the truth. There is no decrease in the degree of importance, instead, there is a shift in the role played. This shift may place the teacher in an even more important position. Concerning the preceding discussion of knowledge, it seems reasonable to expect the quality of students' inquiry and discovery to be enhanced with the expert participation of the teacher.

Thelen indicates that, as a facilitator, the teacher must encourage inquiry. This responsibility can be divided into the following three segments: 1) stimulating inquiry and investigation; 2) arranging for individuals and small groups to interact at thinking and feeling levels; and 3) guiding reflective thinking to build deeper meanings and clearer values.

Questions which help children explore divergent thinking, such as open-ended questions, function as a major tool in the inquiry process. *Example:* Instead of indicating to students that they will need jars, dirt, and seed for a particular experiment, it is much more effective to pose the question "What problems do you observe, and what materials do you think you will need to explore them?" *Example:* Instead of reporting that the ball rolled up the inclined plane instead of down because of the effect of the "center of gravity," etc., it enhances desire to inquire and discover if the teacher merely asks, "How can you explain that?"

It is certainly not implied that the students will discover scientific truths that have taken experienced scientists many years to discover, but students will arrive at answers. Answers coupled with validity testing will lead to learning, possibly not facts as described by textbooks, but learning of processes which can lead to empirical knowledge.

Evaluation Continuous, involves teacher and student.

Traditionally, paper and pencil tests have been the instruments used for evaluation purposes. The results of these tests have been used to compare the performance of one student against that of another student or an established standard. The notion that students should be compared to an arbitrary set standard or a group norm has no validity in the open space classroom. It is often reiterated that all students are individuals with varying capacities, abilities, and potentials. Therefore, students must be evaluated on the basis of their particular potential for growth and development. Any other standard would be invalid because each student is unique in every attribute. The open space classroom is dedicated to enhancement of differences and the development of human potential. Teachers see students in a state of creative growth, instead of moving in a predetermined path. When the comparison of scores between two individuals is assumed to be no longer valid, new evaluation procedures must be contrived. The first step in the development of new evaluation procedures is the involvement of students.

A starting place for this involvement may be the pupil-teacher conference. As stated previously, student self-direction is a major objective of the open space classroom. Self-direction can be thought of as a composite of four components:

1. Student assessment of his behavior, attitudes, ability, and other pertinent information about himself.
2. Planning on the basis of the assessment.
3. Decision-making regarding the implementation of this plan.
4. Evaluation of the effectiveness of the plan.

In the student-teacher conference, both parties cooperatively assess the student's effectiveness in performing these functions. In this process, the teacher must interact honestly and realistically with her pupils and encourage them to do the same.

Suggestions for student-teacher conference. If a student does have a problem in any particular type of learning (cognitive or affective), he should be encouraged to suggest a solution. If the student cannot or does not suggest a solution, the teacher may offer some of the following:

1. Work with a partner temporarily if the current assignment is difficult but apparently appropriate for him at this time.
2. Select a more appropriate assignment for the student.
3. Ask the student to seek the aid of the librarian or another student temporarily until his reference skills can be improved.
4. Ask the student to survey the areas of the room where materials are located.
5. Gather information on the number of unnecessary interruptions of students taking place in the classroom. (The principal, field consultant, or aide could assist in the information gathering. . . .)
6. Suggest that the student move to a more appropriate area (perhaps the quiet study area).
7. Redefine area standard with small groups of students in the class.

8. Suggest that a student go on to another activity if the AV equipment or material is not available at the time rather than wait. He can do this later or go to another subject area.

9. Adjust his contract for completion of assignment. (California Teacher Development Project, 1970, Fremont, Ca.)

As a result of the counseling session, the changes might have to be of a more comprehensive nature. For example, the very immature student who is having difficulty attending to any task for more than a few minutes needs much support from the teacher until he achieves successful experiences. When this success occurs, gradual withdrawal of support, while the student maintains the same level of achievement and success, is possible. This change involves an extensive effort on the part of the teacher but has the potential of bringing about a comprehensive change in the student behavior.

An affective behavior checklist of student performance is presented below. This instrument can be used for recording student behaviors. The information recorded can be used by the teacher and student in planning activities and solutions that will aid the student in his development of self-direction. Behaviors may be added or deleted by the individual teacher so that the checklist is characteristic of her stated goals.[1]

________________ ________________

Student's Name Date

CHECKLIST OF STUDENT PERFORMANCE
Affective Behavior

Carrying Through On Tasks With Responsibility And Effort

________A. Started self-assigned or teacher-assigned tasks promptly.

________B. Carried out task without reminder.

________C. Completed learning tasks or play activities in spite of interference from other students.

________D. Did thorough job on task.

________E. Continued beyond requirements of task.

________F. Made efficient use of AV media or books.

______G. Planned a strategy or a schedule involving several tasks.

______H. Completed a strategy involving several tasks.

Showing Independence And Initiative

______A. Worked out satisfactory solution when faced by unfamiliar or unexpected situation.

______B. Developed appropriate solution for required activities previously reported as uninteresting.

______C. Verbally demonstrated independent thinking in face of verbal opposition to his ideas.

______D. Asked teacher or fellow student questions in an attempt to relate current content to previously learned concepts.

______E. Sought additional work or asked to make up work.

______F. Made up poem, song, or carried out original project.

______G. Voluntarily worked on task or tried to learn a special skill which was not a required assignment.

Comments ____

____

These 15 behaviors relate to a student's performance in the classroom. During the conference, the teacher and student can discuss which of these behaviors are occurring and check (√) those behaviors. The remaining behaviors, those with no checkmarks, are the ones that need to be encouraged.

Other unique evaluation procedures may be found in Kohl (1969, pp. 106-112) and Howes (1968, pp. 98-100).

Individualized Instruction

As stated previously, individualization is the vehicle or means through which the objectives of open space are realized. It is crucial then that individualized instruction be examined in close detail.

Many and various definitions have been offered for individualized instruction; possibly the most accurate definition is providing appropriate learning experiences for individuals. Regardless of the definition chosen, individualized instruction involves four basic elements: pacing, objectives, materials, and personalization. The elements are dealt with in their respective order.

Pacing

Attempt at individualization most often occurs in the mathematics and reading areas. A logical reason for this emphasis is the sequential nature of these subject areas. These sequences can be envisioned as a continuum with the less complex concepts at one end acting as prerequisites to the more complex concepts at the other end. This sequential nature makes these subject matters easily adaptable to the elements of individualized pacing. The process is something like this. Through diagnostic precedures, students are assigned to a concept on the continuum that represents the edge of their knowledge in that subject area. Individuals then progress along the continuum at paces commensurate with their attitudes, abilities, and other pertinent factors. Individualized pacing may involve little more than segmenting the textbook into a sequence of objectives (concepts) and posting this information so that students may use it as a syllabus.

There are prerequisites to a successful individualized pacing program. The first is student orientation. To work efficiently in this type of program, students must be introduced to the procedures before the program is implemented. Even after the program has been implemented, the first few weeks must be considered as a learning experience and a period of adjustment. Record keeping is another factor that must be considered. The progress of students must be monitored so that accurate reports can be made to parents and so that students may be organized for instruction on the basis of need.

Objectives

Often times, individualized programs contain the same objectives for each student. In areas such as mathematics and reading, it is particularly difficult to individualize objectives since it is assumed that all students must learn to read, add, subtract, and divide, etc. Although the concept to be learned is the same for all students, some aspects of behavioral objectives are easily adapted to individual differences. Let us demonstrate.

The student will compute on paper, after three learning activities and a conference with the teacher, the answers to ten problems, such as the following, within ten minutes and with no errors:

$$26\overline{)487}$$

Consider the previous objective as consisting of the following elements: (1) the doer; (2) overt behavior; (3) results; (4) given conditions; and (5) standard of acceptable performance. In the preceding objective, the doer is the "student," the overt behavior is "compute on paper," the results are "answers," the given conditions are "three learning activities, ten minutes, one teacher conference and on paper," and the standard of acceptable performance is "no errors." With this format in mind, the differentiation of objectives to meet individual differences becomes more convenient. For instance, the doer, the overt behavior, and the results are constant, but the given conditions and the standard of acceptable performance are easily changed. For some students, the given condition may be 20 minutes, four learning activities, and a conference with the teacher. The standard may be changed to 80 percent or even 70 percent and 20 instead of 10 minutes. In areas such as science, social studies, and health where the structure is not necessarily sequential, the entire objective (all five elements) may vary from student to student. These areas provide students the opportunity of selecting or even writing their own objectives.

Materials

Materials, as with objectives, are often more difficult to individualize than pacing. There is an obvious cause for this dilemma. Often, the only instructional materials purchased for mathematics or reading classes are textbooks; frequently, the same textbook is purchased for every student. Textbooks are very useful instructional tools, but in an individualized classroom, students will be working on different objectives requiring various types of materials. For this reason, furnishing identical texts for all students is not a sound pedagogical practice. Providing instructional materials appropriate for every student requires ingenuity and creativity. Any games or textbooks written on different levels of sophistication can aid in individualizing. Sharing materials with other classrooms also helps.

When considering the three types of resources: (1) *physical*— textbooks, etc.; (2) *institutional*— parks, zoos, etc.; and (3) *hu-*

man; we see that textbooks (physical) and teachers (human) are the two types of instructional resources generally employed. Institutional resources are seldom used because of expense, inconvenience and/or inapplicability. Textbooks are often used because they are plentiful. Teachers serve as the human instructional resource because they are available, but teachers are overburdened in this respect. Other human resources are available to provide instructional assistance. Students can often provide this assistance quite nicely. Pupil tutoring is an instructional technique and resource that is seldom tapped. Students may be grouped on the basis of need in the affective, psychomotor, and cognitive areas so that the best match may be attained. This tutoring practice can take place within the individual classroom, or it might involve cross-age grouping with other classrooms in the school.

Personalization

The last, but definitely not the least important, element is the personalized instruction provided by the teacher. Children have different learning styles and personality characteristics that must be considered in evaluation procedures and when providing instruction. To constantly emphasize the auditory mode when the child learns best through the visual mode or to treat the aggressive child in the same manner as the retiring child is certainly not sound pedagogy. Types of thinking processes also need to be considered; deductive and inductive thought processes are examples. These two styles can be altered to better fit the learning strength of the child. In addition to learning styles and dominant cognitive processes, the degree of independence each child can efficiently manage must also be considered. For example, some children may require continuous assistance from the teacher in order to fit the "parts" together to form the "whole," while others may be capable of making discoveries quite independently. In this case, the teacher needs to provide only a minimum of direction. To personalize instruction, factors such as those just mentioned need to be considered and individualized for each child. To truly individualize instruction, all four elements must be individualized. Many individualized or self-pacing programs parade under the guise of total individualization. Individualized pacing means just that, students proceed through curricular sequences at paces commensurate with their attitudes and abilities. This is sound pedagogical practice, but without including objectives, materials, and personalization, true individualization does not exist. These elements can exist independently; individualizing one does not necessarily individualize another.

Procedures

A student's activity in an individualized program is often much different than a student's activity in a more conventional classroom. As stated previously, this activity is often independent, not teacher directed. A paradigm representing student activity in an individualized program is presented in Figure 2.

The model indicates numerous situations where students may channel or be channeled into different avenues as determined by their individual performance.

1. After taking the pre-assessment test and interpreting the results three avenues are possible.
    a. review prerequisite skills needed for efficient attainment of the new objective,
    b. engage in a learning activity as determined by the objective and the student's learning style, and
    c. engage in extended learning activity to develop breadth of understanding of current concept or advance to next objective in the sequence.
2. After taking the post-assessment and interpreting the results, two avenues are possible.
    a. engage in another learning activity that develops the same concept if objective was not attained on first try, or
    b. advance to next objective in the sequence or engage in an extended learning activity to develop breadth of understanding of current concept.

If one student is working through the sequence presented in Figure 2 or if all students are progressing through the sequence as a group, then the teacher would be performing the same functions for nearly all students at any given time and in a set sequence. In an individualized program, students are working at various stages in the sequence at the same time; therefore, the teacher must perform different functions at various times and in no set sequence. Teacher activities are also presented in Figure 2.

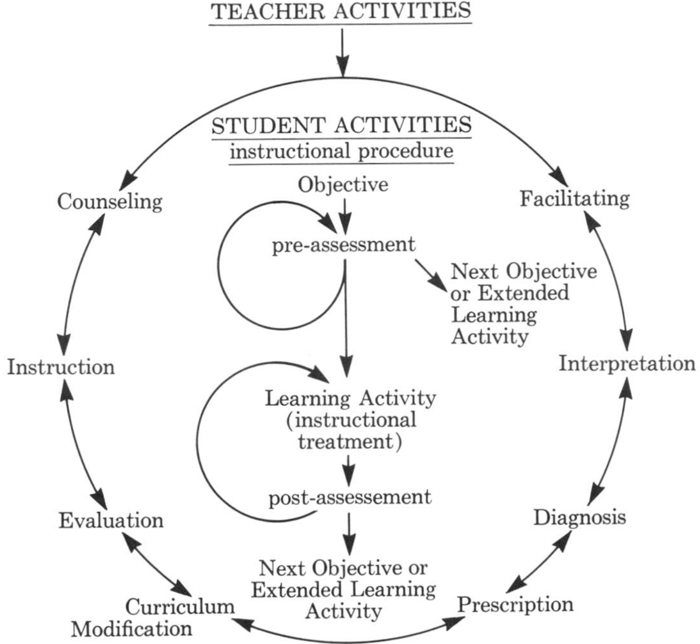

Figure 2. *Instructional Procedures — Teacher and Student Activity*

Teacher Concerns and Difficulties

As illustrated in the opening paragraph, teachers often fear the prospect of open space and rightfully so; many questions must be answered. A few of these questions and concerns are discussed on the following pages.

Student Control

When talking to teachers who have attempted to create open space, one can detect a common thread in their advice, "Start the program off gradually!"An attempt to create an open space classroom in one day or in one week is sure to end in disaster. After functioning in a relatively autocratic classroom, students are generally not accustomed to decision-making. Consequently, when one tries to develop an open space classroom, students are often bewildered and frustrated. At times, they *insist* on being directed, or they tend to misuse their new freedom.

The following three suggestions may be helpful in developing your open space classroom:

1. Responsible decision-making takes time, patience, and an acceptance of mistakes. To begin this process, allow students to make a few more decisions than they are normally accustomed to. Let students select, or give students an assignment that covers two or three days instead of one. The child must schedule his time and activities in this situation or face failure in completing his assignment. The student's first try may not be successful, but with counseling, planning, time, and confidence, the student is likely to demonstrate success.

2. Teachers have intuitive notions about how responsible students are. Select those students who are likely to be successful in handling self-responsibility, and let them work independently throughout the day or in a number of activities. Indicate to other students that when they feel as though they would like to accept the responsibility for directing themselves, they may do so after discussing it with the teacher. The key to this technique is enforcing the verbal contract. When a child fails to use his time wisely, he must be denied his freedom to direct himself.

3. A more complicated approach is to let the students develop classroom rules and regulations. In this technique, as in the first two, teacher sincerity is crucial to success. When rules and regulations are determined by the teacher and students, they must be enforced until changed by a democratic procedure. A valid reason for changing a rule may be undue hardship on any one or a number of people in the classroom. Autocratic teacher procedures are hazardous; they communicate insincerity to students. Implementing this procedure with just one segment of the day is advised over beginning with the entire day.

In summary, student commitment (self-responsibility/self-direction) will solve student control problems for the teacher and teacher aide in the development of a successful open space classroom, but these affective behaviors cannot be learned without the freedom to experience such situations. A practical hint for developing student self-commitment is taken from social psychology.

A study of consumer behavior in soda fountains showed that the sales would increase dramatically if customers were asked one type of question, and sales decreased if the questions were asked in a different way. For example, sales went up if the customer was asked, "Would you like a large or small coke?" Sales went down if the question was "Would you like a coke?"

The implication is that it is not advisable to offer the child the option of learning or not learning by asking, for instance, "Mary, would you like to work this unit on changing nouns to adjectives?" Rather, the choice offered the student should be to select from among different units. For example, "John, which of these three units in biology would you like to explore — the unit on man, animals, or plants?"

Conclusion

The following quote by Kohl summarizes many teacher concerns and attitudes that are crucial to the success of open space:

> An open classroom develops through the actions of the teacher and not because of his words. . . . It took at least a year for me to be at ease in my classroom and to stop worrying about what was supposed to happen and start reacting directly to what was actually happening. Nothing developed magically; freedom and openness are not formulas for success. . . . To have a free classroom is to present an environment where many people can discover themselves, and there is no simple set of rules to prescribe how this can be created.[2]

To determine your open space index, record your answer in the appropriate blank to the left of each question.

YES	NO	
______	______	1. Are my classroom procedures conducive to student self-direction?
______	______	2. Are my behaviors, such as my facial expressions when asking and answering questions, conducive to student self-respect?
______	______	3. Do my instructional techniques generally allow for active student participation (discovery and inquiry) rather than passive listening?
______	______	4. Do I group and regroup students on the basis of need?
______	______	5. Do my classroom procedures allow students experiences in decision-making?
______	______	6. Do I provide students opportunities to assume responsibility?
______	______	7. Do I participate in my classroom as a facilitator, guide, and/or resource person rather than an autocratic dispenser of knowledge?
______	______	8. Do I evaluate students on basis of ability rather than comparison to group norm?
______	______	9. Do I use attitude inventories and behavior checklists rather than only objective tests to evaluate my students?
______	______	10. Are grades determined in my classroom through a cooperative student-teacher process?
______	______	11. Do I provide different objectives for different students as determined by need?
______	______	12. Do I allow different amounts of time for different students to complete objectives?
______	______	13. Do I recognize different "learning styles"?

YES	NO	
______	______	14. Do I provide learning materials and activities based on these individual "learning styles"?
______	______	15. Am I willing to accept student misuse of responsibility and freedoms as a critical learning experience in affective development?
______	______	16. Am I willing to let students select and determine a number of objectives?
______	______	17. Do I view the student as an active, sensing, impressionable individual?
______	______	18. Do I recognize affective objectives (attitudes, values) as pertinent and relevant for consideration in my classroom?

Review the content of the questions for which you replied "no." Closely examine the "why" behind your "no" answer. Based on the information provided in this booklet and your professional consideration, re-answer the questions originally marked "no." Now, count your "yes" responses. The more "yes" responses you gave the closer you are to open space.

Plot your open space index on the space continuum below.

CLOSED OPEN

1 2 3 4 5 6 7 8 9 10 11 12 13 14 15 16 17 18

SPACE SPACE

References

Affecting Learning

Glasser, William. *Schools Without Failure.* New York: Harper, 1969.

Mager, Robert F. *Developing Attitude Toward Learning.* Palo Alto: Fearon Publishers, 1968.

Raths, Louis E., Harmin, Merrill, and Simon, Sidney B. *Values and Teaching.* Columbus, Ohio: Charles E. Merrill Publishing Co., 1966.

Rucker, W. R., Arnspiger, A. J., and Brodbeck, A. J. *Human Values In Education*. Dubuque: W. C. Brown Book Co., 1969.

Behavioral Objectives

Armstrong, J. R., Cornell, Terry D., Kraner, R. E., and Roberson, E. W., eds. *Developing and Writing Behavioral Objectives*. Tucson: Educational Innovators Press, Inc., 1968.

Frase, Larry E., and Talbert, Gene E. "Behavioral Objectives: Panacea or Holocaust." *Audiovisual Instruction* 16 (March 1965): 85.

Gronlund, Norman E. *Stating Behavioral Objectives for Classroom Instruction*. Toronto: The Macmillan Company, 1970.

Kibler, R. J.; Barker, L. L., and Miles, D. T. *Behavioral Objectives and Instruction*. Boston: Allyn and Bacon, Inc., 1970.

Mager, Robert F. *Developing Attitude Toward Learning*. Palo Alto: Fearon Publishers, 1968.

Mager, Robert F. *Preparing Instructional Objectives*. Palo Alto: Fearon Publishers 1962.

Classroom Ideas

Bigge, Morris L. *Learning Theories for Teachers*. New York: Harper, 1964 pp. 308-350.

California Teacher Development Project. Fremont, Calif. 1970.

Darrow, Helen F., and Van Allen, R. *Independent Activities for Creative Learning*. Edited by Alice Miel. New York: Teachers College Press, Teachers College, Columbia University, 1967.

Esbenson, Thorwald. *Working with Individualized Instruction*. Palo Alto: Fearon Publishers, 1968.

Howes, V. M., Darrow, H. F., Kerischer, R. E.; and Tyler, L. L. *Exploring Open Structure*. Los Angeles: Educational Inquiry Inc., 1968.

Kohl, H. R. *The Open Classroom*. New York: New York Book Review, 1969.

Mager, Robert F. *Developing Attitude Toward Learning*. Palo Alto: Fearon Publishers, 1968.

Rucker, W. R., Arnspiger, V. C., and Brodbeck, A. J. *Human Values in Education*. Dubuque: Wm. C. Brown Book Co., 1969.

Thelen, Herbert. "Some Classroom Quiddities for People-Oriented Teachers." *Journal of Applied Behavioral Science* Vol. 1, No. 3 (1965): 270-275.

Theory

Benjamin, Harold. *The Saber-tooth Curriculum.* New York: McGraw-Hill Book Co., 1939.

Bishop, Lloyd K. *Individualizing Educational Systems.* New York: Harper, 1971.

Glasser, William. *Schools Without Failure.* New York: Harper, 1969.

Holt, John. *How Children Fail.* New York: Dell Publishing Co., 1964.

Holt, John. *The Underachieving School.* New York: Dell Publishing Co., 1969.

Howes, V. M., Darrow, H. F., Kerischer, R. E., and Tyler, L. L. *Exploring Open Structure.* Los Angeles, Calif.: Educational Inquiry Inc., 1968.

Kohl, H. R. *The Open Classroom.* New York: New York Book Review, 1969.

Leonard, George B. *Education and Ecstasy.* New York: Dell Publishing Co., 1964.

Postman, N. and Weingartner, C. *Teaching As A Subversive Activity.* New York: Delacorte Press, 1969.

Notes

---

[1]*California Teacher Development Project.* Fremont, California, 1970.

[2]Herbert R. Kohl, "The Open Classroom," *The New York Review,* New York 1969, pp. 33, 115.

Howard E. Blake and Ann W. McPherson

Individualized Instruction—Where Are We?

A Guide for Teachers

A question that has been of continuing concern to teachers throughout most of the history of education is how to meet the individual needs of pupils in a school operation which is geared to masses of students. Despite the magnitude of this problem, it is still largely unsolved. The consensus of those who have given serious attention to it seems to be that its solution will require rather massive and long-range research effort.

What is Individualized Instruction?

Individualized instruction means that the learning program for each curriculum area is organized in such a manner as to allow each child to move at his own pace under the guidance of his teacher. Instruction is non-graded, enabling each child to go as far in each subject as his ability permits.

Individualized instruction does not mean the child works alone at all times. It does not mean that the teacher relinquishes his responsibilities to a machine or to teaching materials. While the child works alone more than in traditional classrooms, the teacher has to diagnose his progress frequently and offer him, as well as

Howard E. Blake and Ann W. McPherson, "Individualized Instruction—Where Are We?" *Educational Technology* 9 (December 1969): 63-65.

small groups or the entire class, supplemental instruction where there is a common need.

Children cannot learn effectively through individualized instruction simply by being told to proceed at their own pace through the study of traditional materials. Specially prepared materials are essential. Present experience indicates that a series of projects, worksheets, or lessons are necessary, commencing at the very beginning of each subject and proceeding sequentially until all the content of the subject has been completed.

Current Trends in Individualized Instruction

For about the past ten years there has been a concerted effort to do something about individualizing instruction. Several factors have strengthened this movement.

1. More teaching materials have been developed to enable the teacher to organize his classroom on an individualized basis.
2. We have learned much more in recent years about the process of instruction itself. We have developed experience in producing programs of materials that teach a subject in relation to its basic structure and according to how children learn. We know that children must be involved in their learning and not merely be **told;** that pupil interest is a great factor in learning; that reinforcement and immediate feedback of answers aid learning rate; and that children learn best when allowed to learn at their own pace.
3. Our country has realized that local school districts cannot provide all the financial support necessary for a quality educational program, and has significantly increased its financial support of schools.
4. Teacher-education institutions are preparing a "new breed" of teachers, committed to making schools more challenging for children.
5. The current emphasis on community involvement in schools has led parents to question the value of group-teaching and to demand that their children be provided instructional programs applicable to the children.
6. There is a growing feeling among teachers themselves that they want to individualize instruction.

Schools throughout the nation are currently testing numerous individualized instructional programs of one kind or another. The most notable of these is the project in Individually Prescribed Instruction (IPI) developed at the learning Research and Development Center, University of Pittsburgh.

Offered at the elementary school level in three subjects—mathematics, reading and science—numerous worksheets or lessons have been developed for children to study on an individualized basis.

Frequent diagnosis of a child's progress is made by the teacher, who then writes a "prescription," telling the child which lessons he is to do next. Children study at their own pace, and may proceed as far in the study of each subject as they can.

IPI is currently offered in many selected schools throughout the nation. The Oakleaf Elementary School in Pittsburgh is its demonstration pilot school.

The Duluth, Minnesota, school system has developed its own curriculum for individualization. In that program, each subject area is broken down into a series of sequential contracts which children undertake and complete at their own pace. Other school systems throughout the nation—Dayton, San Francisco, San Mateo, Philadelphia, Washington, D.C.—are engaging in various experimental projects to individualize instruction.

Advantages of Individualized Instruction

The experience gained from these and other programs indicates that individualized instruction has advantages for both the teacher and the child not found in other kinds of teaching.

For the child

— It enables him to proceed at his own pace through the study of each subject.

— There is a one-to-one relationship between him and the subject he is studying.

— It permits him to get an immediate response to his answers; immediate satisfaction is gained.

— It enables him to understand better the structure of the subject he is studying.

— It enables him to study in greater depth those aspects of the subject which diagnostic tests indicate he needs, and to move with greater speed on those materials with which he is more familiar.

— Instruction is non-graded; each child can proceed in a subject as far as his ability will permit.

For the teacher

— It frees the teacher from teaching many of the routine basic skills of a subject.

— It enables him to meet more accurately the instructional needs of each child.

— It furnishes him with diagnostic devices.

— It allows him to spend more time with students who need help the most.

— It enables him to bring a structured, carefully thought-out program to his pupils.

— It brings about a higher degree of job satisfaction.

— It helps the teacher to serve not only as a lecturer, but also as a guide to the pupil.

Hardware vs. Software

The development in recent years of a great amount of technological equipment has made it possible for a different kind of instruction to be offered in schools. The difficulty is that the present machines are more sophisticated than the available teaching materials used with them.

A number of educational and industrial institutions are currently developing instructional materials—the "software"—that are going to have a greater impact on teaching in the immediate future. Equipment technology will be better harnessed, and will be of more help to the teacher.

The Teacher and Individualized Instruction

Some educators take the point of view that individualized instructional programs—both the hardware and the software—will some day take the place of the teacher and eventually make the teacher's role unnecessary. Another frequently heard reaction is that prepared materials dehumanize learning. It is interesting to remember that teachers in the fifteenth century felt the same threats when the printing press was invented.

Individualized programs are but a start in what children must learn. They cannot possibly replace the teacher. Instead, they will take the load off the teacher for teaching much of the basic skills and content, leaving him valuable and much needed time to humanize learning — leading discussions, raising challenging questions, diagnosing, working with individuals, conferences, examining materials, planning, listening to children. Teachers seldom feel they can find enough time to devote to these matters, and this makes teaching frustrating. What better way can we give attention to these important concerns than by finding a way to be relieved of the teaching of a large portion of the basic skills and content?

Not only will individualized instructional programs give the teacher a new status and role in the classroom, but they will bring a new excitement into teaching and learning, making it a truly creative experience for teachers and children.

Good teachers will seek good individualized instructional programs and will develop a philosophy that will enable them to use this approach in their classrooms; for such programs offer the greatest assurance of raising the quality of both teaching and learning.

Ralph W. Tyler

Testing for Accountability

The growing concern about accountability has put new emphasis on measuring what and how much a student has learned in a short period of time. To measure educational outcomes in such a period requires tests designed for this purpose—and the problem for administrators is that most tests currently available are not very suitable.

A good example of the problem is in the area of performance contracting, where schools contract for instruction with private companies on a fee arrangement based on student performance. Since it appears that performance contracts will generally be let to cover students considered to be low achievers from disadvantaged environments, the standard achievement tests in common use do not furnish a dependable measure of how much these children have learned during one school year or less.

They were not constructed to do so.

A typical achievement test is explicitly designed to furnish scores that will arrange the pupils on a line from those most proficient in the subject to those least proficient. The final test questions have been selected from a much larger initial number on the basis of tryouts and are the ones which most sharply distinguished pupils in the tryouts who made high scores on the total test from those

---

Ralph W. Tyler, "Testing for Accountability," *Nations Schools* 86 (December 1970): 37-39.

who made low scores. Test questions were eliminated if most pupils could answer them or if few pupils could answer them, since these did not give much discrimination.

As a result, a large part of the questions retained for the final form of a standard test are those that 40 to 60 per cent of the children were able to answer. There are very few questions that represent the things being learned either by the slower learners or the more advanced ones. If a less advanced student is actually making progress in his learning, the typical standard test furnishes so few questions that represent what he has been learning that it will not afford a dependable measure for him. The same holds true for advanced learners.

This is not a weakness in the test in serving the purpose for which it was designed. The children who made lower scores had generally learned fewer things in this subject than those who made higher scores and could, therefore, be dependably identified as less proficient. Furthermore, a good standard test has been administered to one or more carefully selected samples, usually national, regional or urban samples, of children in the grade for which the test was designed. The scores obtained from these samples provide norms for the test against which a child's score can be related.

These tests — called *norm-referenced tests* — thus provide dependable information about where the child stands in his total test performance in relation to the norm group. But when one seeks to find out whether a student who made a low score has learned certain things during the year, the test does not include enough questions covering the material on which he was working to furnish a dependable answer to that question.

This leads to another problem encountered when one attempts to measure what a child learns in a school year or less. In the primary grades, particularly, each child's learning is dependent on what he had already learned before the year began and what sequence he follows. For example, in reading, some children enter the first grade already able to read simple children's stories and newspaper paragraphs. Measures of what they learn during the first year should be based on samples of reading performance that go beyond this entry level.

On the other extreme, some children enter the first grade with a limited oral vocabulary and without having distinguished the shapes of letters or noted differences in their sounds. Measures of what such a child learns during the first year must take off from his entering performance and be based on the learning sequence used in his school to help him acquire the vocabulary and language skills that are involved in the later stages of reading instruction.

A standardized test, however, is designed to be used in schools throughout the nation, despite the different learning sequences they have and with children coming from a variety of backgrounds and at various stages of learning in the field covered by the test. For this reason, it cannot include enough questions appropriate to each child's stage of development to measure reliably what he has learned during a single school year.

Recognizing that norm-referenced tests can provide dependable information on the relative standing of children, but cannot reliably measure what a child has learned or how much he has learned in a year or less, efforts are now under way to construct and utilize tests that are designed to sample specified knowledge, skills and abilities and to report what the child knows and can do of those matters specified. Since the criterion for a performance contract is that each child will learn specified things, a test that samples them is called a *criterion-referenced* test.

For example, in primary reading, the children who enter without having learned to distinguish letters and sounds might be tested by the end of the year on letter recognition, association of letters with sounds, and word-recognition of 100 most common words. For each of these specified "things to be learned," the child would be presented with a large enough sample of examples to furnish reliable evidence that he could recognize the letters of the alphabet, he could associate the appropriate sounds with each letter, alone and in words, and he could recognize the 100 most common words. A child has demonstrated mastery of specified knowledge, ability or skill when he performs correctly 85 per cent of the time. (Some small allowance, like 15 per cent, is needed for lapses common to all people.)

At a higher level of initial performance, a group of children may be expected to read and comprehend typical newspaper paragraphs, simple directions for making or doing something, etc. Similar specifications are made in arithmetic and in writing. Science and the social studies represent greater problems because of the variations in content and the lack of agreement on essential objectives.

The National Assessment of Educational Progress utilizes criterion-referenced tests and reports to the public about the performance of various categories of children and youth rather than individuals. The public is given the percentage of each group — 9 year olds, 13 year olds, 17 year olds, and young adults — who know certain facts, can use certain principles in explaining phenomena, are able to do certain things. The reports reveal the exercises that were used and give the per cent of each group who answered the question correctly or who demonstrated the ability or skill involved. The public can get a better grasp of what children and youth are learning by these reports than by trying to interpret abstract scores.

The need for criterion-referenced tests is particularly acute when a contractor undertakes to aid the education of disadvantaged children. Currently used standard tests are not satisfactory tools to appraise the learning of disadvantaged children that can be expected in a single school year. Because most of the disadvantaged begin the year at much earlier stages than a majority of pupils, the standard tests developed for that grade include very few questions that represent what these children are learning.

For this reason, when such a test is given at the beginning of the year and a second test at the end of the year, the changes in score for an individual child may largely be chance variations, since both scores are based on very small samples of knowledge, abilities or skills to which these children could respond. Furthermore, since the number of questions on which the initial score is based is small, coaching for these particular items can give a large relative gain. For example, if a child answered four questions correctly in the initial test, being able to answer four more in the final test will place him very much higher on the relative score of a standard test than would a gain of four points when his initial score was 40.

This fact increases the temptation for coaching in the case of contracts involving disadvantaged children. Criterion-referenced tests constructed for the learning sequences actually being followed will include a much larger sample of appropriate questions.

Although there are few criterion-referenced tests presently available, if performance contracting continues to expand rapidly, both schools and contractors will soon recognize that they do not have the tests they need to furnish dependable measures of performance. Publishers may well respond by a crash program of criterion-referenced test development.

Arthur W. Combs

Fostering Self-Direction

SCHOOLS which do not produce self-directed citizens have failed everyone—the student, the profession, and the society they are designed to serve. The goals of modern education cannot be achieved without self-direction. We have created a world in which there is no longer a common body of information which everyone must have. The information explosion has blasted for all time the notion that we can feed all students the same diet. Instead, we have to adopt a cafeteria principle in which we help each student select what he most needs to fulfill his potentialities. This calls for student cooperation and acceptance of major responsibility for his own learning.

As Earl Kelley has suggested, the goal of education in the modern world must be the production of increasing uniqueness. This cannot be achieved in autocratic atmospheres where all decisions are made by the teachers and administration while students are reduced to passive followers of the established patterns. Authoritarian schools are as out of date in the world we live in as the horse and buggy. Such schools cannot hope to achieve our purposes. Worse yet, their existence will almost certainly defeat us.

Arthur W. Combs, "Fostering Self-Direction," *Educational Leadership* 23 (February 1966):373-376.

The world we live in demands self-starting, self-directing citizens capable of independent action. The world is changing so fast we cannot hope to teach each person what he will need to know in twenty years. Our only hope to meet the demands of the future is the production of intelligent, independent people. Even our military establishment, historically the most authoritarian of all, has long since discovered that fact. For twenty years the armed forces have been steadily increasing the degree of responsibility and initiative it expects of even its lowest echelons. The modern war machine cannot be run by automatons. It must be run by *thinking* men.

Much of the curriculum of our current schools is predicated on a concept of learning conceived as the acquisition of right answers and many of our practices mirror this belief. Almost anyone can pick them out. Here are a few which occur to me:

Preoccupation with right answers; insistence upon conformity; cookbook approaches to learning; overconcern for rules and regulations; preoccupation with materials and things instead of people; the solitary approach to learning; the delusion that mistakes are sinful; emphasis on memory rather than learning; emphasis on grades rather than understanding and content details rather than principles.

Meanwhile, psychologists are telling us that learning is a *personal* matter: individual and unique. It is not controlled by the teacher. It can only be accomplished with the cooperation and involvement of the student in the process. Providing students with information is not enough. People rarely misbehave because they do not know any better. The effectiveness of learning must be measured in behavior change: whether students *behave differently* as a consequence of their learning experience. This requires active participation by the student. So learning itself is dependent upon the capacity for self-direction.

Toward Self-Direction

What is needed of us? How can we produce students who are more self-directed?

1. *We Need To Believe This Is Important.* If we do not think self-direction is important, this will not get done. People are too

pressed these days to pay much attention to things that are not important. Everyone does what seems to him to be crucial and urgent. It seems self-evident that independence and self-direction are necessary for our kind of world. Why then has self-direction been given such inadequate attention? It is strange we should have to convince ourselves of its importance.

Unfortunately, because a matter is self-evident is no guarantee that people will really put it into practice. It must somehow be brought into clear figure in the forefront of our striving if it is to affect behavior. Everyone knows it is important to vote, too, yet millions regularly fail to vote. To be effective as an objective, each of us must hold the goal of self-direction clear in our thinking and high in our values whenever we are engaged in planning or teaching of any kind.

This is often not easy to do because self-direction is one of those goals which *everyone* is supposed to be working for. As a result, almost no one regards it as urgent! For each person, his own special duties are so much clearer, so much more pressing and his derelictions so much more glaring if he fails to produce. The goals we hold in common do not redound so immediately to our credit or discredit. They are therefore set aside while we devote our energies to the things that *really* matter to us.

To begin doing something about self-direction we must, therefore, begin by declaring its importance; not as a lofty sentiment, but as an absolute essential. It must be given a place of greater concern than subject matter itself, for a very simple reason: It is far more important than subject matter. Without self-direction no content matters much. It is not enough that it be published in the handbook as a "Goal of Education." Each of us at every level must ask himself: Do I really think self-direction is important and what am I doing about it?

2. *Trust in the Human Organism.* Many of us grew up in a tradition which conceived of man as basically evil and certain to revert to bestial ways if someone did not control him. Modern psychologists tell us this view is no longer tenable. From everything we can observe in humans and animals the basic striving of the organism is inexorably toward health both physical and mental. It is this growth principle on which doctors and psychotherapists depend to make the person well again. If an organism is free to do so—it can, will, it *must* move in positive ways. The organism is not our enemy. It wants the same things we do, the achievement of adequacy. Yet

alas, how few believe this and how timid we are to trust our students with self-direction.

A recent best selling book, *Summerhill,* by A. S. Neill has fascinated many educators. In it Neill describes the absolute trust he placed in the children under his care. Many teachers are shocked by his unorthodox procedures and the extreme behavior of some of the children. But whether one approves of Neill's school or not, the thing which impressed me most was this: Here was a man who dared to trust children far beyond what most of us would be willing to risk. Yet, all the things we are so afraid might happen if we did give them such freedom, never happened! For forty years the school continued to turn out happy, effective citizens as well as, or better than, its competitors. It is time we give up fearing the human organism and learn to trust and use its built-in drives toward self-fulfillment. After all, the organism has had to be pretty tough to survive what we have done to it through the ages.

Responsibility and self-direction are learned. They must be acquired from experiences, from being given opportunities to be self-directing and responsible. You cannot learn to be self-directing if no one permits you to try. Human capacities are strengthened by use but atrophy with disuse. If young people are going to learn self-direction, then it must be through being *given* many opportunities to exercise such self-direction throughout the years they are in school. Someone has observed that our schools are operated on a directly contrary principle. Children are allowed more freedom of choice and self-direction in kindergarten (when they are presumably least able to handle it) and each year thereafter are given less and less, until, by the time they reach college, they are permitted practically no choice at all! This overdraws the case, to be sure, but there is enough truth in the statement to make one uncomfortable. If we are to produce independent, self-starting people, we must do a great deal more to produce the kinds of experiences which will lead to these ends.

3. *The Experimental Attitude.* If we are going to provide young people with increased opportunity for self-direction, we must do it with our eyes open *expecting* them to make mistakes. This is not easy, for the importance of "being right" is in our blood. Education is built on right answers. Wrong ones are regarded as failures to be avoided like the plague. Unfortunately, such attitudes stand squarely in the way of progress toward self-direction and independence.

People too fearful of mistakes cannot risk trying. Without trying, self-direction, creativity and independence cannot be discovered. To be so afraid of mistakes that we kill the desire to try is a tragedy. Autonomy, independence and creativity are the products of being willing to look and eager to try. If we discourage these elements we do so at our peril. In the world we live in, victory is reserved only for the courageous and inventive. It is possible we may lose the game by making mistakes. We will not even get in the game if we are afraid to try.

Experimentation and innovation must be encouraged everywhere in our schools, in teachers as well as students. Each of us needs to be engaged in a continuous process of trying something new. The kind of experimentation which will make the difference to education in the long run is not that produced by the professional researcher with the aid of giant computers but by the everyday changes in goals and processes brought about by the individual teacher in the classroom.

To achieve this, teachers need to be freed of pressures and details by the administration for the exercise of self-direction and creativity. In addition, each of us must accept the challenge and set about a systematic search for the barriers we place in the path of self-direction for ourselves, our colleagues and our students. This should suggest all kinds of places for experimentation where we can begin the encouragement of self-direction. One of the nice things about self-direction is that it does not have to be taught. It only needs to be encouraged and set free to operate.

4. *The Provision of Opportunity*. The basic principle is clear. To produce more self-directed people, it is necessary to give more opportunity to practice self-direction. This means some of us must be willing to give up our traditional prerogatives to make all the decisions. Education must be seen, not as providing right answers, but as confrontation with problems; not imaginary play problems either, but *real* ones in which decisions count.

Experiences calling for decision, independence and self-direction must be the daily diet of children, including such little decisions as what kinds of headings and margins a paper should have and big ones like the courses to be taken next year. They must also include decisions about goals, techniques, time, people, money, meals, rules, and subject matter.

If we are to achieve the objective of greater self-direction, I see no alternative to the fuller acceptance of students into partnership in the educative endeavor. Our modern goal for education, "the optimal development of the individual" cannot be achieved without this. Such an aim requires participation of the student and his wholehearted cooperation in the process. This is not likely to be accomplished unless students have the feeling they matter and their decisions count. Few of us are deeply committed to tasks imposed upon us; and students are not much different. Self-direction is learned from experience. What better, more meaningful experience could be provided than participation in the decisions about one's own life and learning?

The basic belief of democracy is that when people are free they can find their own best ways. Though all of us profess our acceptance of this credo, it is distressing how few of us dare to put it to work. Whatever limits the capacity of our young people to accept both the challenge and the responsibilities of that belief is destructive to all of us. It is time we put this belief to work and to expression in the education of our young as though we really meant it.

II

Individualized Instruction: Teacher Skills

Sadly, for many teachers the price of incorporating individualized instruction and related procedures into their classrooms has been chaos, dismay, and finally, the verdict that individualized instruction is "nice" in theory but not practical, desirable, or even remotely possible in practice. This conclusion is distressing but not true.

Often the reason for the bitter failure that may follow heroic attempts at individualization is the lack of proper and adequate planning. The individualized classroom can and often does appear as undirected, purposeless human interaction to the so-called traditional teacher who "jumped" into individualized instruction. The key to success in individualization is planning and starting small. Teachers must prepare themselves for new student activities. In an individualized classroom, students may be working individually, in small or large groups on varying activities, tutoring each other, selecting, at least partially, their own learning activities, and preparng their own daily schedule. For himself, the teacher must imagine and prepare for a role as a facilitator of learning who diagnoses learning difficulties, prescribes and directs learning activities, implements programs, tutors individuals, directs para-professional help, and counsels with individuals and groups of students. Maybe not all, but some or most of these activities are foreign to the vast majority of today's classrooms.

Most educators recognize the objectives and worth of individualized instruction and its related practices, but few are acquainted with the new skills required of teachers in an individualized classroom. Hopefully, the articles in this section will help teachers plan for the new skills and roles that combine to make teachers facilitators of learning.

Bernice J. Wolfson

Pupil and Teacher Roles In Individualized Instruction

We have been hearing a persistent call for better education. Yet, the people who join in making this appeal are far from agreement in their criticisms of present school conditions and in their views of what is required to effect improvement (1).

"Better education" may mean more up-to-date knowledge, faster achievement, better teachers, introducing new disciplines in the early grades, preparing every child for college, or, less often, changing education to make it more relevant to the lives of today's children. On the one hand, the emphasis may be on "more-and-better" of the school's traditional pattern and role. On the other hand, the focus may be on finding some new pattern for the institution and for the processes to occur within it.

Why Individualize?

With the second focus in mind, many of us in education are committed to the idea of individualizing instruction. Again, we find a variety of reasons for this commitment. Some of us hope to teach

---

Bernice J. Wolfson, "Pupil and Teacher Roles in Individualized Instruction," *The Elementary School Journal* 68 (April 1968): 357-366.

more efficiently than we have taught under some form of group instruction We want children to achieve the same learnings we have been striving for but at different rates and possibly with greater amounts of enrichment. Others want to encourage greater individuality among pupils and a wider variety of learning outcomes. Still others perhaps want to go beyond our current view of the classroom to transform our present goals and ways of working into a new image made possible by individualized instruction. No doubt, there are additional purposes. But it seems to me that each of us must know why he wants to individualize instruction. What makes it a desirable thing to do?

Personally, I believe that individualizing instruction can enable us to change our educational direction. I would like to see less emphasis on conformity and more on initiative and individuality. I would like to see us break out of the box of "covering content" as defined in grade level steps or predetermined sequences. Particularly, I would like to see more opportunities for children to ask questions of real concern to them, to make choices and plans, to evaluate and think independently, and to develop individual interests and commitments. I am well aware that many thoughtful and gifted teachers have sought to provide such opportunities with varying degrees of success. I believe that organizing to individualize instruction — or, more accurately, to encourage personalized learning — will strengthen efforts to move in these directions.

What is Individualization?

Even though we might develop some agreement about reasons for individualizing instruction, our definition of the process is not quite clear. In fact, observations in classrooms where teachers say that they are individualizing instruction reveal a wide variety of practices. Teachers may be using traditional textbooks and workbooks and allowing each child to work at his own pace. Teachers may have conferences with individual children. They may instruct small groups in particular skills. In some classrooms pupils may use programmed materials or textbooks assigned by the teacher on an individual basis, as she decides they are appropriate. In other classrooms small groups of children who share some common interest may work together, and individual children may select their own materials from the available resources.

It is not at all certain that these practices provide individualization. Take a pupil-teacher conference. This procedure obviously provides a one-to-one relationship. But the teacher may be doing the same thing that she would do in a directed reading lesson with a group. In fact, she may be doing what she does with many of the other pupils, one at a time. I would not consider these conferences examples of individualized instruction. The use of programmed learning materials and textbooks with individual pacing is not truly an example of individualized instruction. These materials provide for differences in rate of learning, but are not responsive to other kinds of variation among pupils, such as motivation, style of learning, energy level, attitudes, previous learning, and complex personality factors.

At present, the most popular interpretation of individualized instruction is that the teacher makes specific recommendations and assignments for each pupil. This interpretation rests on the teacher-as-doctor analogy, an analogy seriously in need of examination. According to this view, the teacher functions as a doctor; that is, she diagnoses needs, deficiencies, or problems and prescribes appropriate treatment.

Admittedly there is something appealing about this analogy. Part of its appeal is probably due to the high status doctors have in our society. To say that teachers behave like doctors is therefore seen as a compliment. However, I think that the attractiveness of this analogy is due mostly to the apparent simplicity, precision, and neatness of the model: One assesses the present condition, diagnoses the nature of the problem, prescribes the appropriate treatment, and a cure is effected.

However attractive this model may be, teaching really does not fit such a design. (And I doubt that doctoring does either.) Surely teaching is more complicated than doctoring, has more dimensions, and, in spite of intensive efforts, has not developed clear-cut criteria for treatment success.

Let us examine this model further as it might be applied in a hypothetical classroom. Consider the plight of the teacher who must diagnose and prescribe for thirty pupils in many subject areas over an extensive period of time. Does she really know what each pupil is ready for or what specific learning experiences he needs next? She may have some general hunches, and perhaps she could get some helpful suggestions from the pupil. But how would she make her diagnosis and prescription? She might decide that a pupil is ready for third-grade work or for subtraction or for addition with bridging. She might decide that he needs practice in recognizing beginning sounds. Or she might merely decide that he has successfully completed one section of his workbook and is ready to start the next section. In many so-called non-graded schools she would decide that he is ready to read at Level 11.

Most of these decisions, it seems to me, are arbitrary and often not relevant to the pupil's understanding of his world. Somehow I do not believe that these are meaningful ways of planning for individual, continuous learning. Furthermore, since the teacher is the chief source of evaluation, her relationship with the pupil is necessarily judgmental and the pupil continues to be dependent on her evaluation of his efforts. Finally, the inappropriateness of this model becomes clearer when we recognize that the teacher as a diagnostician is led to focus on needs, disabilities, and problems instead of attending to the pupil as a person who is constantly growing and learning. If the doctor analogy is inappropriate, what analogy might be more fitting?

Recently, I have been exploring the notion that the teacher is more like a travel consultant. Suppose you want to take a trip to the Orient. You tell the travel consultant what you think you would like to see. He will have some questions: How much time do you have? What are you most interested in seeing? How much money do you want to spend on this venture? How do you prefer to travel? He may suggest other possibilities you did not know existed. A good travel consultant will help you to plan loosely, so that you will not find yourself dashing from one place to another. He will also help you to plan flexibly, so that if you find a place that you particularly enjoy you can make arrangements to stay longer.

Among the interesting features of this analogy, at least as far as I have taken it, are the implications for outcomes. It seems to me that this analogy implies that the primary outcome is not simply to get to the Orient. The outcomes are the kinds of experiences you have along the way and while you are there. Some of these outcomes are completely unpredictable — the people you happen to meet, the experiences you could not anticipate. These unpredictable outcomes might be, in the long run, the most vital aspects of your trip — the ones you remember forever, in contrast to the general clear-cut objective of getting to the Orient or of seeing certain sights that you decided on in advance. Furthermore, other travelers can choose other destinations.

This analogy, in contrast to the medical analogy, is in large part open-ended, responsive to persons (rather than to deficiencies), and clearly allows for self-direction. Still, after all has been said, analogies are merely vivid pictures that may help us see new relationships but that necessarily fall short of describing the realities we are discussing. Instead of exploring analogies, then, let us consider how teachers and pupils might function to promote the kind of individualized and personalized learning that is truly responsive to, and supportive of, individuality.

Beliefs We Can Question

For a discussion of this kind we must first eliminate some of the constraints that inhibit our thinking about new roles. These constraints are both conceptual and institutional. The first conceptual constraint I would discard is the idea that there is a necessary sequence for learning certain skills, or a particular set of sequences that is best for all children. Also I would discard the idea that certain predetermined sequences are necessary to develop understanding in a content area. These two assumptions underlie programmed learning and the "structure-of-discipline" approach to curriculum. In addition, I do not believe that we know what knowledge and skills all children should have. Knowledge is neither certain nor permanent. As for skills, I think there are certain agreements in our culture. For example, in order to learn you have to be able to read, and reading involves a variety of interrelated skills. However, there is great difference of opinion as to what constitutes reading skill and how children learn to read. Commonly held assumptions inhibit our view of curriculum.

I would also discard the premise that the learner is primarily a receptive, reactive organism responding to stimuli presented by the teacher and by teaching materials, as well as to reward and punishment, or approval and disapproval, as meted out by the teacher. I would reject the view, still common among teachers, that intelligence tests measure the child's ability, or potential for learning, and that this potential is fixed and almost entirely genetically determined. Assumptions of this kind limit our perceptions of children.

I disagree with those who believe that grade level is a meaningful and useful way of organizing schools and curriculums. I do not believe that the teacher directly controls what is learned by the class. Nor do I believe that certain specific content or concepts must be covered during a school year. Finally, I cannot accept the current conviction that specific behavioral objectives provide the best guidelines for the planning of teaching and learning.

All these commonly accepted assumptions can, I believe, be challenged and rejected. Here I will discuss only the first assumption: that there is a best or desirable sequence for learning.

A study by Mager (2) raises some interesting questions about learning sequence. Six adults were studying electronics in a learner-directed program. Each subject in this study was treated individually and took part in one to seven sessions that lasted sixty-five minutes on the average.

In the experimental group, the instructor's role was merely to respond to the questions and requests of the learner. These requests could be for information, for demonstration, for reviews, for whatever the learner felt he needed at the moment.

Some interesting findings emerged. The author reported: "Subject-matter commonality in the learner-generated sequences was greatest at the outset of instruction. As instruction progressed the learners moved into their areas of special interest in electronics. . . . The instructor-generated sequences began with an entirely different topic than did the learner-generated sequences. This suggests that the sequence most meaningful to the learner is different from the sequence guessed by the instructor to be most meaningful to the learner" (2:3). In fact each learner pursued a different path of instruction. The instructor found it difficult to follow the questions of the learner. Mager commented: "If the instructor finds it difficult to keep up when the sequencing of content is controlled by the student, what kinds of obstacles must the student be facing when the instructor controls the sequence?" (2:3).

Also, although the subjects were convinced that they knew absolutely nothing about electronics before this experiment, it turned out that they actually had a large body of relevant background information from which the instructor could draw. In addition, from the learners' behavior, the way they raised questions and used the information they got, it appeared that they "were continously attempting to tie new information to information they already knew, whether correct or incorrect" (2:3).

Finally, the author concluded, "The data suggest that the learner's motivation increases as a function of his control, or apparent control, of the learning situation. Subjects' comments indicated that they terminated their sessions because they felt unable to absorb more material rather than because they were bored" (2: 3).

Mager started out to compare the effectiveness of instruction using the traditional methods with the effectiveness of instruction using programmed materials. He found that he saved time when he used the program. However, he saved even more time when he used learner-directed instruction. This investigation, it seems to me, encourages us at least to question the conviction that we can determine the best sequence for teaching and learning (3).

Roles Redefined

A willingness to question many commonly held assumptions will make it possible to visualize a new model of the classroom. We must, of course, be aware that the same actions at different times and in different contexts will have different meanings. We cannot say that behaving in a certain fashion is necessarily consistent with our goal of developing individuality. Furthermore, each classroom is a unique environment for learning. It could not be otherwise. Each teacher is unique, and each combination of individuals who make up a class is unique. The resultant mix of personalities, attitudes, interests, resources, and materials can never be duplicated.

How then might pupils and teachers, having discarded the old assumptions, function in these environments? I will describe some possible roles that I believe would encourage the individual development of the pupil.

Principally, the pupil could play a more significant role in determining his learning activities. He could be involved in significant decisions — not just in the unimportant ones we usually allocate to him. Within broad limits, he could choose what he will learn and in whose company. He could plan and evaluate for himself. He could be free to raise questions important to him and to explore his world outside the classroom as part of his planned learning. He could be encouraged to clarify his personal meanings and values. In short, he could be a self-directing, active learner, a role not often emphasized in today's schools.

The teacher's role would be primarily that of consultant and resource person to the learner. She would be a manager of the classroom environment, supplying a variety of materials and at times initiating new experiences. She would help pupils learn to plan, to evaluate, and to consider alternatives. She would bring her own interests and inquiry into the classroom. The main focus of her activity would be to promote self-direction (4). Of course, each teacher's approach is unique. But if a teacher does not intend to promote self-direction, she will not truly allow children to make choices. Her intent, therefore, will influence how she and her pupils organize their class.

In these classrooms there would be a flexible mix of individual activities, small-group activities, and large-group activities. There would be frequent pupil-teacher conferences. Small groups might ask the teacher to confer with them. Temporary interest-centered groups would develop and disband as they completed their plans. At times the entire class would meet at the request of the teacher or a pupil. A wide variety of materials in many media would be available. Resources outside the classroom would also be used. The significant element in organizing and using resources would be the co-operative planning of pupils and teacher.

A word of caution is appropriate here. Many of the features I have been describing may be found in classrooms that are not focused on the educational purposes I have been emphasizing. Furthermore, we cannot conclude that the presence of these features will in themselves further individualized instruction and the development of self-direction. The intent and the functioning of the teacher will have an important influence on the pupils. Are they actually learning to be self-directing, or are they merely learning how to give the teacher what she expects? The teacher's attitudes, values, perceptions, and communications contribute to the formation of classroom climate and to the pupil's perception of his role in school.

New Roles in Action

Let us turn now to some examples of efforts to achieve the type of educational experience I have been discussing. Three projects seem to me to incorporate the spirit of this conception. There are undoubtedly other examples.

The first project was reported in an article called "Mississippi's Freedom Schools: The Politics of Education." In that article Florence Howe described her experience as a teacher and director of a Freedom School one August. Most of her work was with a group of eleven- to fourteen-year-olds. Her description seems to communicate the realities of the situation. Take the following remarks about the teacher role:

> The teacher's main problem was to learn to keep quiet, to learn how to listen and to question creatively rather than to talk at the students. He had to discard whatever formal classroom procedures he had ever learned and respond with feeling and imagination as well as with intelligence and good humor to the moods and needs of the group. Above all, the students challenged his honesty: he could not sidestep upleasantness; he could not afford to miss any opportunity for discussing differences [5:155].

These comments, it seems to me, convey an awareness of the need for "real" people as teachers. They also remind us that teaching consists of confronting problems. One cannot support a particular approach to teaching in the hope that it will eliminate all problems. Teachers and pupils must choose to confront the problems that they feel are meaningful. These are not necessarily the problems that other people consider meaningful.

A second example of an effort to achieve the type of educational experience I have been describing is an experimental high school in California. A report of the first year of the school describes the problems and the development of a school designed for "maximum student involvement and maximum freedom for individual growth" (6: 1). In discussing curriculum and the related teacher-student roles the authors state:

> In the classroom, the student is shown that he should feel free to be himself. Our teachers try not to hide behind their teacher role; they, in turn, urge students not to hide behind theirs. They *all* begin their courses as students, the teachers only perhaps farther along in their questioning. Teachers encourage their students to formulate and share their own questions. By sharing in the inquiry, students will hopefully be drawn by their own natural curiosities into a search for the heart of each subject, and to the basic questions which draw disciplines together. They are made free to explore . . . the student learns to take more and more charge over his own education. By making choices available, by encouraging individual and small-group projects, by fostering an open, non-threatening atmosphere, by encouraging divergence of approach and opinion, by allowing ample room for unscheduled exploration, by aiding in the formation of individual goals, and by giving each student some personal attention and understanding, the teacher in the classroom makes constructive use of the individual learning pattern and goals of each student [6:4].

In this description, too, we can see an awareness of the need for teachers to be "real" people to their students. Admittedly, it is easy to describe an experimental school in glowing terms without providing corroborative evidence of its practices. I have spoken with the writers of this report, but I have not yet observed the school in action. Still, the direction of the effort clearly speaks to the kind of possibilities I am exploring.

For a third example, I would like to describe some observations made by teachers with whom I have been working, who teach in multiage, heterogeneous classrooms. As you can imagine, working with randomly assigned six-, seven-, and eight-year-olds (or nine-, ten-, and eleven-year-olds) in one classroom requires one to individualize instruction and to provide a wide variety of materials and learning opportunities.

In some of these classrooms I have seen evidence of extensive changes in teacher and pupil roles Some teachers report that they experience a new kind of relationship with their pupils. At times, as pupils become increasingly self-directing, the teachers wonder how much they are needed. They note that pupils feel free to come to the teacher for help on various problems, but often the pupils also seek help from other pupils. Teachers express amazement at the capabilities of some of their pupils, capabilities that were completely unexpected. Some teachers also report that they do relatively little direct instruction, and are surprised to see growth in skills on achievement tests without specific instruction.

In these classes pupils appear to learn to accept differences in other children and to work willingly with individuals who would ordinarily be in other grades. Many pupils pursue individual or small-group projects for an extensive period. One boy at the primary level spent much time studying continents and then proceeded to study air currents. Two boys (who would have been in third and fourth grade in a traditional organization) worked together for a long time studying about various animals.

I could give many examples (4) but to describe what one may see in a class of this kind, or to describe the activities a teacher and her pupils engage in, does not get to the heart of the matter. To provide the type of environment for learning I have been trying to describe, the teacher must have a view of man, and of children in particular, that allows her to see them as growing creatively, rather than as moving in predetermined paths. She must be able to interact honestly and realistically with her pupils. Living in schools can be real, not just playing the game of beating the system. To me individual and personalized learning means really living in school.

Help from Research

There is little research on the conception I have tried to develop. Most current research about teaching seems to me to be based on a mechanistic rather than an organismic model of man. The classroom observation and analysis research done in recent years by Anderson, Withall, Flanders, Smith, Hughes, Medley and Mitzels, and others (7) have produced observation and category systems that purport to describe and analyze the teacher's behavior, mostly verbal behavior. The result of these efforts is a relatively superficial labeling or categorizing of the teacher's verbal acts. These categories describe a limited dimension of teaching behavior, but they are not really pertinent to what the teacher thinks she is doing. Nor are they particularly crucial dimensions of the teacher's actions. It seems to me that this type of analysis is equivalent to using the linear dimensions of an automobile and the names of some of its parts in an effort to describe and explain its functioning. Research of this kind assumes that the teacher's verbal behavior is meaningfully described by discrete units of activities in categories such as "asks questions" or "accepts feelings." This research also assumes that these bits, when added together in each category and examined for proportional distribution, will characterize some significant differences among teachers.

I have no objection to researchers who observe teaching and try to describe and even measure what they see. I would hope they might uncover some meaningful relationships. However, for the teacher of teachers and for the teacher herself, study of this kind has not yet yielded much useful information. I have already suggested that these studies fail because of the mechanistic nature of their analysis. I would also like to suggest that it is a mistake for the teacher to look to research for specific answers to her concerns as a practitioner. Like the aesthetician, who may possibly add to the artist's generalized thinking about art, but not directly affect how he goes about creating a painting, the student and researcher of teaching may possibly add to our generalized understanding about teaching, but not directly affect how we go about teaching.

How Teachers Know

It seems to me that our most vital questions as teachers cannot, at least at present, be answered by the researcher, the curriculum specialist, or the principal. Each of us must draw our working answers from our personal interpretation and integration of our current knowledge and experience. Indeed, our "tacit knowledge" (8) guides our actions whether in wisdom or in error.

I would like to close with the reminder that science is but one way of knowing, no doubt an extremely useful way but still, as Bronowski said, uncertain. Bronowski went on to say:

> Not all experience is got by observing nature. There is a second mode of knowledge which differs from the procedures of science. In our relations with people, and even with animals, we understand their actions and motives because we have at some time shared them, so that we know them from the inside. We know what anger is, we learn an accent or the value of friendship, by directly entering into the experience. And by identifying ourselves with the experience of others, we enlarge our knowledge of ourselves as human beings: we gain self-knowledge [9:83].

In my view of individualized and personalized learning, the teacher is working with her knowledge from the inside as well as with her observations from the outside. It is, I believe, through some combination of both kinds of knowledge that we must continue to search for the heart of the matter in struggling with the concepts of teaching and learning I have been discussing. The teacher cannot relinquish either focus, or indeed separate them, if she is concerned with her own and her pupils' personal learning.

Notes

1. This article is based on a paper originally presented at a Workshop on Individualized Instruction, University of California, Los Angeles, July, 1967.

2. Robert R. Mager. "On the Sequencing of Instructional Content," reported by Millicent Alter in *Programed Instruction 4* (November 1964), 3-4.

3. See: Robert F. Mager and John McCann. "Learner-controlled Instruction." Palo Alto, California: Varian Associates, 1961.
Robert F. Mager and C. Clark. "Explorations in Student-controlled Instruction," *Psychological Reports 13* (August 1963), 71-76.
Vincent N. Campbell and Madalynne A. Chapman. "Learner Control vs. Program Control of Instruction," *Psychology in the Schools 4* (April 1967), 121-30.

4. Bernice J. Wolfson, "The Promise of Multiage Grouping for Individualizing Instruction," *Elementary School Journal 67* (April 1967), 354-62.

5. Florence Howe. "Mississippi's Freedom Schools: The Politics of Education," *Harvard Educational Review 35* (Spring 1965), 144-60.

6. Raymond J. Roberts and Carolyn Schuetz. "Monte Vista High School — The First Year." San Ramon Valley Unified School District, Danville, California, 1966. (Mimeographed.)

7. Nathan L. Gage. *Handbook of Research on Teaching.* Chicago: Rand McNally and Company, 1963.

8. Michael Polanyi. *The Tacit Dimension.* Garden City, New York: Doubleday and Company, 1966.

9. J. Bronowski. *The Identity of Man.* Garden City, New York: The Natural History Press, 1966.

Madeline Hunter

When the Teacher Diagnoses Learning

WHAT kind of a boy is Johnny? What has he already learned? What "next" learning tasks are appropriate for him? How can a teacher increase the efficiency and economy of his accomplishment?

As the teacher confronts these questions for each learner under his supervision, small wonder he is tempted to murmur, "Please pass the crystal ball!" Fortunately, crystal balls and divining rods are not available on supply requisition lists, so professional rigor is beginning to replace folklore and fantasy as the basis for diagnosis of and for educational prescription for the learner.

This shift from routinized application of the currently recommended panacea (what is it this year, look-say or phonics?) to decision making based on critical evaluation of each learner has been the major factor in the change from the technology of teaching to the profession of education.

No longer is diagnosis restricted to or reserved for only the educationally "sick." Rather, such diagnosis has become an intrinsic part of the teaching act for *all* learners. Out of such diagnosis are created educational prescriptions. The repertoire of competencies of the teacher and alternatives offered by the school constitute a pharmacy from which such prescriptions are filled.

Madeline Hunter, "When the Teacher Diagnoses Learning," *Educational Leadership* 23 (7) (April 1966): 545-9.

We first must identify the questions such diagnosis is designed to answer. Only then can we seek instruments whose validity, reliability and precision give us confidence in the accuracy of the assessment on which diagnosis is based.

Diagnostic Questions

Identification of the essential and relevant has as its irrefutable and logical counterpart identification of the nonessential and irrelevant. The latter, no matter how fascinating and tempting (with *that* home situation what can you expect of me?), must be discarded. We also must discard many of our most easily collected but relatively worthless "test results" on learners.

Each datum we use in our diagnostic procedure must pass the screen of contributing to the answer to one of the following questions:

1. What objective is appropriate for this learner to achieve? (Notice the change from "*I* am seeking to attain with this learner.")
2. What is his present status in relation to that objective?
3. What is the next learning step in attainment of that objective?
4. Based on data about this learner, what can the teacher do to help him take that step efficiently and economically?
5. Was he successful?
6. If so, what is the next appropriate step?
7. If not, what changes should be made?

Questions 1, 2 and 3, are content-based. Knowledge of the learning task (reading, math, or ball playing) must be related to the assessment of the learner's present degree of achievement.

Question 4 is learner-based. An assessment of the intellectual, physical, social, and emotional factors that contribute to or detract from the learning process provides the data for the answer.

Questions 5, 6, 7 are evaluation-based, where "at this moment in time" must become the qualifying phrase for any answer.

Let us begin with an inspection of these questions as they relate to a physical activity so we will not get trapped in the value-imbued educational platitudes ("competency in reading," "appreciation of the democratic process"), which are so emotionally charged. Suppose we are trying to determine the appropriate high jump objective for a boy of a given age. The first factor that becomes obvious is that other data may be more critical than his age. Does he have long or short legs? Is he fat or thin? How well is he muscled and coordinated? (It makes you stop to reconsider the statement that ten-year-old boys should be reading at a fifth grade level, does it not?)

Suppose we agree that this boy should be able to clear a five-foot bar. Now we turn to our second question—how high can he actually jump? We find (possibly to our horror) that he can comfortably clear only a 3′ 8″ bar, although on occasions he can jump a 4′ one. Obviously, at this point we are not going to insist he keep trying the 5′ bar, but plan to start teaching so he can consistently clear the 4′ one. (Hammering away at 5th grade work that is too difficult is as obviously unsound.)

Our fourth question is concerned with the use of data about the learner that will guide us in planning the learning opportunity and teaching strategy to help him accomplish his task. Will competition with other jumpers stimulate or retard his effort? What for him is the optimum ratio of success or failure? If he responds well to performance heavily weighted with success, we had better keep the bar at 3′ 10″. If he is motivated by the frustration of some failure, let us start at 4′. What does he need in the way of teacher support? Shall we stand by to encourage or let him work by himself? Does he respond well to his own perception of growth or does he need public recognition of his achievement? Will his parents contribute to his achievement motivation or do they think high jumping is a waste of time? (His parents may be getting a divorce or his father may be an alcoholic; however, these dramatic bits of information are not relevant unless we find evidence that they contribute to or detract from his accomplishment of the learning task.)

Now that we have defined the task, and applied a teaching strategy to help him accomplish it, did it work? If the answer is "yes," we are ready to move on to the next task, raise the height of the bar and proceed. If the answer is "no," we must look for factors that may need to be changed. Have we correctly assessed his jumping ability or should we have started with a lower bar? Could there be something wrong of which we were not aware (fatigue, low energy, movement or coordination difficulties)? Was our teaching strategy ineffective? Should we have given more encouragement? Should we have been "tougher" and insisted he "get at it" with consequences if he did not? Would making him the high-jump coach for less able jumpers do the trick? Are there other factors operating which we had not taken into consideration? By practicing, he may miss the opportunity to talk with fascinating girls or perhaps he may be attempting to insure our continued attention by his lack of success.

Our estimate of the correct answer to all of these diagnostic questions becomes the basis for an adjusted educational prescription. Again we fill the prescription from the pharmacy of teaching competency and the alternatives possible in the school and again assess its effectiveness by the performance of the jumper.

Diagnosis in Reading

Let us now pose these same questions in the diagnosis of a learner we find in every clasroom.

Bill is not performing well in reading. While not so remedial that he needs special help, he is dragging at the bottom of his group. We have the uncomfortable feeling that the only thing he is learning is that reading is a bore to be avoided whenever possible.

We begin our diagnosis with the first question, "What goal is appropriate for this learner?" Notice by using goal in the singular, we are being forced to give priority to "enjoyment of reading" *or* "skills in reading" *or* "appreciation of literature" *or* "more active participation in the reading program." Once we identify the primary goal we are able to deal with or eliminate the incompatibility of other goals. (Chaucer and enjoyment may not be compatible at this point.) Unidentified, their counter-directions can neutralize our teaching efforts.

If we select "enjoyment of reading" as the goal basic to the achievement of all others, this becomes our criterion for answering subsequent questions. (It also eliminates such temptations as having his dad make him read an hour each night.)

Our second question, "What is his present status in relation to that goal?" involves a valid assessment of Bill. The eyes and ears of a well prepared teacher continue to be among the best instruments of appraisal; however, we can validate or supplement these observations with objective tests. There is a relationship (but not one to one correspondence) between enjoyment of and skill in an activity, so we need carefully to assess Bill's reading skills. We look beyond the homogenized 5.3 grade placement score on the fact sheet of a reading test because the information we are seeking is inside the test and we will find it only if we inspect Bill's responses.

What kinds of items did he miss? Did he do the easy ones correctly and then quit? Were careless errors responsible for missing easy items while he passed harder ones? Could his errors indicate an attempt to respond correctly or was he simply filling in the blanks? Most important, how does his test performance compare with our daily perception of him? If he performs significantly better in either the test or classroom, what factors might be responsible? Obviously, a numerical grade placement score does not begin to answer these questions.

Let us assume our answer is: Bill *can* read 5th grade material with understanding but the vocabulary load slows him down. Fourth grade material insures a more comfortable pace; however, the content of both 4th and 5th grade material he finds uninteresting. When the reading is difficult he seems to turn off his effort and make wild guesses. When the content is uninteresting, he withdraws into daydreaming with a resultant lack of focus on the learning task.

Our assessment of Bill's performance should direct us to the answer to the question, "What is the next appropriate learning step?"

Now we have two criteria to guide us. The material must be easy enough to encourage his progress and interesting enough to hold his focus. This may involve abandoning, for a time, the state series and selecting a book with a low vocabulary load and exciting content. Remember, "enjoyment of reading" is the goal with highest priority at this point in time. (We are adjusting the high jump bar so he can get over it.) We have not abandoned word attack skills and extraction of meaning, but we are concentrating on first things first.

Having selected an appropriate task, we now turn to our design to help him accomplish it. Here our diagnosis of the learner requires professional literacy in learning theory and personality theory. To what reward system will he respond? Will his accomplishment be positively reinforcing or do we need to add the social rewards of praise and recognition? Do we need to suppress any behavior (such as avoidance of reading) by negative reinforcement? Will *in*creasing or *de*creasing anxiety result in better motivation? How long a reading period can he tolerate before negative feelings take over? How might we extend this period?

These are samples of the questions we must answer for a valid diagnosis. The questions determine whether we skillfully entice him into the reading task or arbitrarily assign it with a time limit and consequences. We may make him the star performer in a book review or may quietly converse with him when the rest of the group are busy. We may make reading a definite assignment or a leisure-time activity. We may "keep after him" or turn him loose.

Diagnosis must lead to action. As mere intellectual exercise it is useless. Consequently, based on our best judgment, we will do *something.* The results determine the validity of our diagnosis and prescription. If all goes well, we will proceed to the next learning task. If not, we will reassess our answers to each of the questions, revise our diagnosis and prescription, and try again.

Many people are seeking an instrument that will diagnose, then will "tell us what to do." It is important that we remember this has not been accomplished in any profession that deals with the intricacies of a human being. The thermometer registers with considerable accuracy the temperature of the patient, but a doctor must decide which medication to use. In spite of his best and learned judgment, some patients are allergic to the dose, and some are beyond his ability to help. Still we have seen tremendous advances in the skill and precision of the medical diagnostician.

As educators, we too are increasing the skill and precision of our assessment of the learner, so we no longer need to keep interminable records and stockpile useless data to stuff cumulative folders. By identification of the critical elements of an assessment we may be sure that instruments will be devised so their objectivity and precision will augment but never replace the highly trained observation that guides educational decisions.

Frank Riessman

Styles of Learning

In any classroom, probably no two pupils learn the same things in the same way at the same pace. Some learn most easily through reading; others through listening; still others through doing things physically. Some prefer to work under the pressure of deadlines and tests; others like a more leisurely pace. Some learn by being challenged by people ahead of them; others learn best by helping people behind them.

Everyone has a distinct style of learning, as individual as his personality. These styles may be categorized principally as visual (reading), aural (listening), or physical (doing things), although any one person may use more than one. Some persons, for example, find it much easier to pace the floor while reading an assignment than to sit perfectly still at a desk. Their style may be more physical.

A common characteristic of the disadvantaged child is his physical approach to learning. He has been exposed to very little reading because his parents rarely have the time to read to him. For this reason, it may be easier for him to learn to read by acting out the words than by hearing them spoken by his teacher. This is borne out by the fact that children at a school in one of New York City's poorest neighborhoods are learning to read effectively by singing and dancing to the words. Since songs and physical move-

---

Frank Riessman, "Styles of Learning," *NEA Journal* 60 (March 1966): 15-17.

ment have been incorporated into the teaching of reading, the percentage of retarded readers in the school has reportedly been cut in half.

For a long time now, teachers and guidance workers have tended to ignore the concept of different styles of learning. They have, instead, focused their attention on emotion, motivation, and personality as causes for learning or failure to learn. When confronted with an intellectually able student whose learning fails to measure up to his learning potential, they have tended to attribute this failure to an emotional block or personality conflict. Little attention has been given to how a pupil's learning could be improved simply by concentrating on the way he works and learns.

I believe that a careful analysis of the way a child works and learns is of greater value than speculation about his emotional state. He may indeed feel sibling rivalry or certain irrational fears, but these conditions may not affect his learning as much as the methods his teacher uses to teach him. The important consideration, in my opinion, is whether the methods of learning imposed by the teacher utilize sufficiently the strengths in a child's style of learning.

Most teachers, unfortunately, have been trained to look upon learning in a general way. Their preparation, which may include no more than a few survey courses in educational psychology, neglects the idiosyncracies involved in learning.

For example, most teachers probably assume that the best way to study a reading assignment is first to survey the chapter. This is what they have been taught from the early grades through college because it is the way most people learn best. Some students, however, become so anxious and disturbed at being told to take an overall view of a chapter that they cannot function. Their style calls for reading a chapter slowly, section by section. Requiring such a person to skim the entire chapter first makes no more sense than telling a person who can't resist peeking at the last chapter of a mystery that he must read the book straight through.

The general recommendation that one must have a quiet place to study may be equally lacking in validity. Strangely enough, some people do their best studying in a noisy place, or with certain sound such as music or even traffic in the background. The textbooks do not talk about this because, for the "average" person, peace and quiet are more conducive to learning.

Style is also very much involved in taking tests. For some individuals, the prospect of a test operates as a prod that stimulates them to absorb a great deal of material they need to master. On the other hand, being faced with a test causes many people to become disorganized, overanxious, and unable to work. After a test, some pupils are so upset over their mistakes that they develop an emotional block about remembering the correct answers to the questions on which they erred. Consequently, they repeatedly miss the same questions. For others, finding out that they gave wrong answers aids recall and challenges them to master the problems.

Each classroom is likely to include students whose styles of learning vary widely. Although the teacher cannot cater completely to each student's particular style, he can attempt to utilize the strengths and reduce or modify the weaknesses of those in his classes.

An individual's basic style of learning is probably laid down early in life and is not subject to fundamental change. For example, a pupil who likes to learn by listening and speaking (aural style) is unlikely to change completely and become an outstanding reader. I am not suggesting that such a pupil will not learn to read and write fluently but rather that his best, most permanent learning is likely to continue to come from listening and speaking.

Since the student is the person most vitally concerned, the first step is to help him discover his particular style of learning and recognize its strengths and limitations.

In identifying a style, it is extremely important to ascertain the person's work habits as precisely as possible. If a youngster is in despair because he cannot get any work done during the study time allowed in class or in the study hall, teachers should question him carefully about his routine. What does he do first when study time is announced? How does he try to make himself concentrate? What disturbs him?

Perhaps his answer will be: "At first I'm glad we have time to do the work at school so that I will be free when school is out. I open my book to the assignment, but it's noisy because kids are asking the teacher questions or flipping through their books or whispering. I go sharpen my pencils while I'm waiting for it to get quiet.

"By the time things settle down, I know I don't have too much time left and that I have to hurry or I won't get done. I try to read fast, but the words all run together and mean nothing. Some of the smart kids are already through, and I haven't even started. I usually give up and decide I may as well do it all at home like all the other dumb bunnies do."

A number of things may be involved in this boy's problem. Possibly he is a physical learner (sharpening the pencils may show some need for movement) who has difficulty with visual learning. Apparently he warms up slowly and works slowly, for when he tries to hurry, he finds he can do nothing.

The physical learner generally gets his muscles into his work, and this takes time. Such a student must realize that attempts to rush himself are of no avail, but that this does not make him a "dumb bunny." Once he gets past his warm-up point and begins to concentrate on his work, he may work very well for long periods of time.

If this student is made aware of the way he learns, he can schedule any work requiring concentration for longer periods of time, and use short periods for something less demanding, perhaps a review of the day's schoolwork. Probably his warm-up period will gradually decrease as he becomes less anxious about failing to keep pace with his fellow students.

A pupil can take advantage of the strengths inherent in his style of learning to balance his weaknesses. For example, consider the pupil who has to learn to read, although his learning style is physical rather than visual.

In order to teach reading to a youngster for whom reading is stylistically uncongenial, the teacher may want to try role playing, which is related to a physical style of learning. The pupil is more likely to be able to read about something that he just role played.

By teaching reading in this way, the teacher is not helping the pupil develop a reading style; he is helping the pupil develop a reading skill.

In a sense, the teacher is overcoming the pupil's difficulty with reading by making use of the pupil's strength, whether it be physical, aural, or whatever.

The challenge to every teacher is first how to identify the learning strengths in his pupils and then how to utilize them to overcome weaknesses. This is the central problem in the strategy of style.

Jeannette Veatch

Individualizing Teacher-Pupil Conferences

Two major questions help teachers understand the how, when, and why of individualization. These are:

1. *When does a teacher teach directly?*
2. *When does a teacher set a situation and let learning happen?*

Instruction

There are times, it seems to me, when a teacher must *instruct*. There are uncountable items in various areas that children will never figure out for themselves even though the habit of wanting to know, of being curious, of asking questions has been highly developed. At any school level, there has to be a place for expert knowledge. The teacher can be the expert or find someone who is.

As I said last month, diagnostic operations help those who would tee off direct "learnin'." Thus such a teacher finds out what a child does not know, and teaches *that*, regardless of whether children are working singly, in groups, or in whole classes.

Jeannette Veatch, "Individualizing Teacher-Pupil Conferences," *Instructor* 75 (January 1966):25-26.

Ground Rules for Conferences

Individual conferences, of course, are the best way to meet individual differences, but a teacher can waste valuable classroom time unless she makes a few rules and observes them.

1. Confer on a sample of a child's total work in a given area. You do not need to see everything each child does. Assume that a good job done on this sample will find the rest of the work at approximately the same level.
2. Let the sample be in some way the child's choice, for then he is personally committed to the learning. What the child brings may reveal an area of need you will recognize if he does not.
3. Work on types of problems or needs. What a child believes he needs may be a sign pointing out a greater need. As you consider a specific question or problem, think what type of learning is indicated.
4. Keep conferences open-ended. The most fair arrangement isn't necessarily to give every child the same amount of time. One child may always need more of your time than another. The same child will need more time on one occasion than on another. If openendedness is achieved, the bright child will not be doing more than he needs to do in a given area and the slow child will not keep trying to catch up with much brighter ones.
5. Let the child feel your personal interest. Exciting teaching and genuine learning can never come through materials alone.

Special Curriculum Areas

Individual conferences may be held in respect to any area of the curriculum. But a conference is most easily set up after children have been exploring a vast array of material. For example:

In *arithmetic*, a teacher should know what to do next with individual children after watching them count or manipulate or, as I saw recently in an English educational film,[1] follow directions on "Order Cards."

In *written composition*, a child chooses, once a week or so, a piece of written material (uncorrected!) from the week's accumulation to bring to his teacher. He may recognize his general need to improve his composition or he may ask specific information related to spelling or punctuation.[2]

In *reading*, the child discusses a portion of a book he helped select and has been reading silently.[3]

Bridgeheads

In closing this series on Individualizing, it seems best to list some bridgeheads that apply to this most crucial teaching operation, regardless of curriculum area. There seem to be four of these.

1. Ask one or more questions that bring a response to the overall, general learning under discussion. In *reading*, questions will probe for central thought and inference. In *writing*, something about the scope or extent of the idea underlying the composition should be asked. In *arithmetic*, the questions will explore the meaning of number at whatever level the child reveals. In *social studies*, a question leading back to the problem statement of the unit helps.
2. Find out why this particular matter which he has brought to the conference especially interests the individual. "Why did you pick this for our conference?"
3. Explore the mechanics of learning as it pertains to the area under discussion. ("How did you get this or that? How do you think you can find out ....?" "How did you get out of trouble when you were stuck?" "Where did you look for the answer?")
4. Give your conferee a chance to demonstrate a skill, display a piece of work, or perform an experiment. He has the right to a place in the sun of teacher recognition. Sensible handling will not produce a braggart.

Finally

Individualization is not a method. It is a way to manage a classroom so that each child has his share of the teacher. Teaching is a human act. It fades when it is dehumanized. Children whose individual differences are truly met will be better taught—because of these differences and not in spite of them.

Notes

1. *I Do and I Understand* (Nuffield Foundation of Modern Mathematics, Sound Service, Ltd., Wilton Crescent, Merton Park, S.W. 19, England). To rent, check with your AV coordinator.

2. For greater detail, see "Mechanics in Written English," by Alvina Treut Burrows, in *The Instructor* (March 1962) and "Functional Spelling" by the same author in *Individualizing Education* (Association for Childhood Education International, 3615 Wisconsin Ave., N.W., Washington, D.C. 20016.

3. The reader is directed to an excellent interim report, "Three-year Longitudinal Study Comparing Individualized and Basal Reading Programs at the Primary Level," by Lakeshore Curriculum Study Council, 2114 E. Kenwood Blvd., Milwaukee, Wis. 53211.

Phelps Wilkins

Record-Keeping Techniques for use in Individualized Instruction

Individualized instruction is one of those ideas in education which almost all educators have eulogized for many years. Yet, the elementary school classroom of the present is very little different from the classroom of 1900, despite the great increase of knowledge about children and how they learn. The typical classroom is still dominated by the teacher who sees his role as soothsayer, manipulator of children, and dispenser of knowledge. Typical classroom instructional methods are based on the textbook and, despite individual student differences, are still oriented toward the average.

Why does educational instructional methodology continue to be oriented primarily towards the group average? What prohibits and retards the realization of personalized instruction? There are many possible reasons why personalized instruction has not attained the utopian state envisioned by some educators. One major reason is the lack of teacher training in personalized instruction methodologies, specifically in the use of information storage and retrieval systems. It is to this point that this paper is addressed.

Personalized instruction can be defined as being a composite of the following characteristics: self-pacing, student and teacher interaction, instruction based on diagnosis and past performance, and the flexibility and ability to employ appropriate media for basic and remedial sequences.

If personalized instruction, as defined, is to operate within the framework of mass education, then each classroom, school, and school district must develop information storage and retrieval systems. The great demands for information storage and retrieval which accompany an individualized program make the development of a data management system essential. The success of individualized pacing, placement, and selection of instructional experiences will depend on the ability of data management systems to provide the needed information on request.

Information storage and retrieval systems vary from highly sophisticated computer installations to simpler record sheets kept in a notebook or file. No one system can best meet the needs of all schools. Each classroom or school must choose or develop its own system. Curriculum design, school objectives, school size, organizational patterns, time-space model, and money available are some of the variables which each school must consider when developing an information storage and retrieval system.

Although the systems will vary from school to school the following questions must be answered:

1. What information is to be stored in the system? Although schools will vary in data storage needs, most would find it useful to include the following:

I. Student characteristics
   A. Aptitudes
   B. Achievement
   C. Interests
   D. Personality (self-image, etc.)
   E. Occupational desires

II. Achievement data
   A. Test scores on unit tests
   B. Test scores for specific performance objectives
   C. Test performance compared to aptitude

2. For what purpose is the information to be used? This is an important question because the uses of the information will determine the organization used to store the information. The methods of retrieval will also depend on its uses. Take for example, Case A: The teacher wants to group all children whose progress indicates readiness to learn how to add fractions. The data to be retrieved are the names of all students who have completed the prerequisite skills necessary to learn addition of fractions. In this case, the data needed must be organized by specific skills in arithmetic. Case B: The teacher needs to identify those students who learn best by the

kinesthetic mode. In this case, the data needed must be organized by learning styles. The system which will allow for data to be grouped many ways is much more useful. The following are some ways schools might use the data:

1. to indicate present performance level along the curriculum continuum;
2. to match students on basis of interests, needs, or abilities for team learning;
3. for weekly or semi-weekly grouping of children for instruction based on need for help with a given skill or concept, attitudes towards math, and learning styles;
4. to group children with special problems, such as visual perception or psychomotor problems; and
5. progress reports to parents.

3. How will the information be put into the system? What personnel are available to store and retrieve data when necessary? The time and talent needed to keep the data bank current will vary according to the system. Some computer systems, after programming, require little additional time from the teacher. Students are often able to feed their own data into the computer. The computer will then analyze, store, and print out data when requested by the teacher.

Other systems often require a great deal of extra time by the teacher or other personnel. Clerical aides are often necessary in order to keep data current.

4. What kind of system is financially feasible? Some systems are extremely expensive while others are relatively inexpensive. The expensive systems, such as computer systems, are often the most versatile. Computer systems not only require costly hardware but also require the services of a programmer to program the computer and to keep it updated.

Other programs, such as file systems, cost little in the way of equipment but often require additional personnel to maintain current data.

Some systems are inexpensive and can be kept updated by the teacher. These systems are usually very limited in their storage capacity and methods of retrieval.

Another important point to consider is the sophistication of the staff in personalized instruction. Expensive storage and retrieval systems are of little value if they are not used. Teachers must be highly trained in order to use the data as efficiently as the computer system can deliver.

5. What information storage and retrieval systems are available that might be used in the classroom or school? The following paragraphs will discuss some of the systems available. These systems have been used successfully both in school and the business world.

Computer Systems

Computer programs have been developed that will do the following:

1. Score and report results of unit tests.
2. Enable the student's performance on test to be compared with his aptitudes, achievements, interests, personal characteristics and background, and preferences for specific occupational and educational groups.
3. List the unit objectives appropriate for the individual student's tentative long-range goals.
4. Compare the student's characteristics in terms of learning style, basic abilities, and special aptitudes with those from the available six or eight teaching-learning units with a particular teaching-learning unit. The analysis is made in terms of whether students with specific learning characteristics can learn effectively by using the particular unit (1).

A computer program such as the one just described can do many tasks quickly and with little effort, but the cost of the hardware and programmer has made it prohibitive for most schools.

McBee Keysort System

A unique low-cost data management system that could be used in the schools is the McBee Keysort system (2). The McBee system allows for a quantity of record sheets to be sorted by any desired factor or into numerical or alphabetical sequence. Equipment and training needed are minimal and inexpensive. The McBee card comes in three sizes 3½″ by 7½″, 5″ by 8″, and 8″ by 10½″.

1	2	3	4	5	6	7	1	3	4	7	1	2	3	4	5	6	7	8	9	10	11	1	2	3	4	5	6
years in school							age				learning exp. level											learning style					

1 2 3 4 5 6 7 8 9 10 11 12 13 14 15 16 17 18 19 20 21 22

Arithmetic Performance Objectives

ARITHMETIC PERFORMANCE OBJECTIVES
1. Addition Facts
2. Associative Property of Addition
3. Adding Three or More Addends
4. Adding Large Numbers
5. Subtraction Facts
6. etc.

LEARNING STYLES (Spec
1. Problems with large muscle coordination
2. Problems with eye-hand coordination

MECHANICS OF LANGUAGE OBJECTIVES
1. Beginning and ending sentences
2. Using commas in words in a series
3. Using commas in dates
4. etc.

NAME____________________________

Figure 1.

Other equipment needed are a punch, sorting needle, alignment block, and card saver.

A keysort card has a series of holes around its perimeter. When notched, these holes allow for the sorting of the cards which contain the desired data.

Coding

Each student is assigned a card. Coding the cards is accomplished by using a hand punch. Each hole is coded to represent certain factors. Each student's card is notched according to the factors which are pertinent to that student.

Sorting

Sorting is accomplished by inserting the keysort needle through the hole representing the desired factor then — lifting. Since wanted cards have been notched in this position, they will immediately fall away from the rest of the deck.

Figure 1 is a brief example of the way keysort cards might be coded.

Files and Notebooks

A system that is inexpensive and that can be kept up-to-date by the teacher or by a clerical aide is a system using record sheets that are kept in a file or notebook. These systems though inexpensive do not lend themselves to quick information retrieval. In spite of this drawback, they have been used by many teachers successfully and are adaptable to specific classroom situations. Record sheets developed by a group of teachers at Holmes School in Mesa, Arizona, are presented in Figures 2 and 3.

Summary

This paper has touched on only a few of the many information storage and retrieval systems a teacher or school might use. Each school is unique and must consider its population size, objectives, organizational pattern, and other variables when designing information storage and retrieval systems.

Notes

1. John C. Flanagan, "Functional Education for the '70's," *Phi Delta Kappan* 49 (September 1967) :27-32.

2. Can be obtained from Automated Business Systems, Division of Litton Industries, 600 Washington Ave., Callstadt, New Jersey 07072.

NAME ____________

GRAPHS	AREA & VOLUME			RATIO & PROPORTION			PER CENT							METRIC SYSTEMS				
EVAL.	143	144	EVAL.	145	146	EVAL.	147	148	149	150	151	152	EVAL.	153	154	155	156	EVAL.
	C	C		C	C		C	C	C	C	C	C		C	C	C	C	

DIAGNOSTIC TEST	ENRICHMENT MATERIALS							
DATE ______ SCORE ______								
DATE ______ SCORE ______								

SPELLING

BOOK	1	2	3	4	5	REV.	7	8	9	10	11	REV.	13	14	15	16	17		19	20	21	22	23	REV.	25	26
NO.	T	T	T	T	T		T	T	T	T	T		T	T	T	T	T		T	T	T	T	T		T	T

27	28	29	REV.	31	32	33	34	35	REV.
T	T	T	T	T	T	T	T	T	

BOOK	1	2	3	4	5	REV	7	8	9	10	11	REV.	13	14	15
NO.	T	T	T	T	T		T	T	T	T	T		T	T	T

16	17	REV	19	20	21	22	23	REV	25	26	27	28	29	REV	31	32	33	34	35	REV	DIAGNOSTIC TEST
T	T		T	T	T	T	T		T	T	T	T	T		T	T	T	T	T		DATE SCORE (PRE) DATE SCORE (POST)

SOCIAL STUDIES

1. ____________
2. ____________
3. ____________
4. ____________

MAP SKILLS

☐ DIRECTIONS ON MAPS
☐ MAP AND GLOBE SYMBOLS
☐ MAP SCALES

LISTENING SKILLS

☐ FOR DIRECTIONS
☐ FOR INFORMATION
☐ FOR COURTESY

RESEARCH & LANGUAGE SKILLS

1 2 3 4

☐☐☐☐ NOTE TAKING
☐☐☐☐ OUTLININC
☐☐☐☐ PROPER FORM
☐☐☐☐ CORRECT SENTENCES
☐☐☐☐ CORRECT PARAGRAPHS
☐☐☐☐ PROPER PUNCTUATION
☐☐☐☐ BIBLIOGRAPHY

REPORTING SKILLS

☐☐☐☐ CLEARLY PRESENTS IDEAS
☐☐☐☐ USES VISUAL AIDS
☐☐☐☐ EVIDENCE OF RESEARCH

READING

PERFORMANCE LEVEL

Date______Level______
Date______Level______
Date______Level______

SKILLS

Deficiencies__________

READING RATE

Date______Rate______
Date______Rate______

LEARNING EXPECTENCY LEVEL

DATE ______MATH______READING______

SCIENCE

PROJECT__________
PROJECT__________
PROJECT__________
PROJECT__________

SELF DIRECTION ☐ ☐ ☐ ☐
SELF RESPECT ☐ ☐ ☐ ☐

NUMBER OF CONFERENCES

☐ 2 ☐ 4

NAME____________ YEAR IN SCHOOL 4 5 6 7 19____ 19____

Figure 2.

UNDERSTANDING NUMBERS					ADDITION OF WHOLE NUMBERS									SUBTRACTION OF WHOLE NUMBERS				
1	2	3	4	EVAL.	5	6	7	8	9	10	11	12	EVAL	13	14	15	16	17
C	C	C	C	C	C	C	C	C	C	C	C	C		C	C		C	

			MULTIPLICATION OF WHOLE NUMBERS												DIVISION OF WHOLE NUMBERS			
18	19	EVAL.	20	21	22	23	24	25	26	27	28	29	30	EVAL.	31	32	33	34
C	C		C	C	C	C	C	C	C	C	C	C	C		C	C	C	C

WHOLE NUMBERS					PROBLEM SOLVING				MEASUREMENT									
35	36	37	38	EVAL.	39	40	41		42	43	44	45	46	47	48	49	50	EVAL.
C	C	C	C		C	C	C		C	C	C	C	C	C	C	C	C	C

UNDERSTANDING WHOLE NUMBERS						ADDITION OF WHOLE NUMBERS					SUBTRACTION OF WHOLE			MULTIPLICATION OF WHOLE				
51	52	53	54	55	EVAL.	56	57	58	59	EVAL.	60	61	EVAL.	62	63	64	EVAL.	65
					C	C	C	C	C	C	C	C		C	C	C	C	C

DIVISION OF WHOLE NUMBERS					MEASUREMENT							PROBLEM SOLVING			GEOMETRY			
66	67	68	69	EVAL.	70	71	72	73	74	75	EVAL.	76	77	EVAL.	78	79	EVAL.	80
C	C	C	C		C	C	C	C	C	C		C	C		C	C		C

UNDERSTANDING FRACTIONS							ADDITION & SUBTRACTION OF FRACTIONS											
81	82	83	84	85	86	EVAL.	87	88	89	90	91	92	93	94	95	96	97	EVAL.
C	C	C	C	C	C	C	C	C	C	C	C	C	C	C	C	C	C	

ADDITION & SUBTRACTION OF DECIMALS						ADD. & SUB. OF WHOLE NUMBERS				MULT. OF WHOLE NUMBERS				DIVISION OF WHOLE NUMBERS				
98	99	100	101	102	EVAL.	103	104	105	EVAL.	106	107	108	EVAL.	109	110	111	EVAL.	
C	C	C	C	C		C	C	C		C	C	C		C	C	C		C

MULTIPLICATION OF FRACTIONS					DIVISION OF FRACTIONS						MEASUREMENT							
113	114	115	116	EVAL.	117	118	119	120	121	EVAL.	122	123	124	125	126	127	EVAL.	128
C	C	C	C		C	C	C	C	C		C	C	C	C	C	C		C

PROBLEMSOLVING		ADD. & SUB. OF DECIMALS			MULT. OF DECIMALS				DIVISION OF DECIMALS			GEOMETRY				SCALE DRAWINGS &		
129	EVAL.	130	131	EVAL.	132	133	134	EVAL.	135	136	EVAL.	137	138	139	EVAL.	140	141	142
C		C	C		C	C	C		C	C		C	C	C	C	C	C	C

NAME____________________________

Figure 3.

Dorris M. Lee

Do We Group in an Individualized Program?

"Hi. Bill! Did you see the notice on the bulletin board? Jim and Kathy are going to discuss Jean Lee Latham's book, *Carry on, Mr. Bowditch,*[1] this morning about 10:00. You wanted to find out about how sailors use sea charts and maps. Let's join the group."

And at 10:05 five boys and three girls join Jim and Kathy in the story-sharing corner of the room. Jim starts by giving the setting and general focus, with an introduction of the main characters and the part they play in the story. Kathy develops the main theme and gives some personal reactions to the author's style and the feeling of reality she has about the characters. Then Jim explains what he has learned about using charts and maps at sea, which is what Bill has joined the group to hear. He begins asking Jim questions about it. Others join in, some with questions, some with comments, and two of them suggest further sources they have found helpful. Kathy then comments on what she has found about Jean Lee Latham's background on this topic and her other biographies. At this point some of the group begins to drift away and back to activities with which they are now more vitally concerned.

Dorris M. Lee, "Do We Group in an Individualized Program?" *Childhood Education* 45 (December 1968): 197-199.

Of course there is grouping in an individualized program! The groups are just formed differently, for different purposes, and continue for different lengths of time. But first we must make clear what we consider individualized instruction to be. *Since* a learning situation, to be effective, must be such that each child can bring personal meaning to it, the child must have at least a part in the planning and decision-making. *Since* each learns in his own way and from the framework of his own present understandings, each must have a part in determining his own procedures for learning. Thus individualized instruction of necessity must involve self-directed learning.

Self-directed learning is a far cry from the justly feared do-whatever-you-want variety. Here the learner identifies his own educational needs, decides what he can do to meet them and how he can most effectively carry out his purposes. The teacher may help as little as by raising a question or as much as by extended conferencing. Planning with children helps them learn how to identify needs and procedures in terms of purposes. Individual conferences, in which the teacher can talk with each child about how he can identify needed learnings and how he decides what procedures would meet his purposes, are most useful in developing self-direction.

What Is a Group?

In this context, what is a group? It is those children who at that time have common specific concerns, needs, interests or plans. It may be initiated by one or more of the children involved or by the teacher or by the interaction of teacher and children. The group stays together as long as the specific reason for its establishment still exists. Some children may leave and others join as their immediate needs are met or developed.

Groups in which children have a part in deciding their participation or which grow out of self-directed activity have values that do not accrue from teacher-established and maintained groups. Almost by definition, there is involvement and purpose not otherwise possible. This eagerness and singlemindedness develop unique learnings. Self-selection of an individual or group learning activity brings commitment attained in no other way. The child then feels a responsibility to himself or the group.

• Mr. Swanson finds that Suzy, Bob, Karen, and Billy have difficulty recognizing base words in derived words. Each one also has become aware that he has not yet learned this, mainly through his or her individual conference with Mr. Swanson. So the group is formed to work together with the teacher in clarifying the problem, each suggesting ways of solving it from his own perceptions and reactions. One child after another gains insight, feels he understands, and leaves the group. With only Bob left, the teacher explores *his* thoughts and perceptions related to base and derived words. He discovers that he has always thought "base" meant "bottom" and never really has been able to bring any meaning to the word in this context. Each time he has thought he understood from the examples, he has become confused by the term. Mr. Swanson clears the meaning and Bob moves another step forward.

Purposes for Grouping

Individuals are unique and, while broadly speaking most have common general needs, immediate and specific needs and concerns differ widely. We believe content is primarily for use in developing concepts and understandings about the world of people and things in which the child lives. Further, we believe that a great variety of content may be used to develop needed concepts and understandings. Since children learn most effectively when dealing with material and ideas to which they can bring personal meaning, they will be using a wide variety of content. The number identifying with certain specific content at any one time may vary from one to possibly eight or ten. If the whole group has had a particularly meaningful experience, they may all want to discuss and think together for a while at least. Groups then provide a vehicle whereby those who can relate well to certain content or ideas may work together in a way most meaningful to them.

• A sixth-grade class has been having a variety of experiences that have oriented them to South America's problems, weaknesses, strengths and concerns; to its climates and general geography; to the languages of its people. Their familiarity with names of countries has alerted the children to comments relevant to South American situations in newspapers and magazines, on TV and radio, and by parents and friends. One morning Sarah comes in with a clipping relating the concern of American meat packers to the importation of Argentine beef. She asked her mother about it and in the store that afternoon they checked the canned meat shelves in their grocery store. Now she wants to know more about it. Her questions and concerns attract several others and a group of six expresses interest in finding out what it means to cattlemen both in the United States and Argentina. Since the teacher believes that a study in depth of one or two countries provides more real understanding, as well as develops skills in tackling a problem to find answers, she encourages the group to go ahead. She also recognizes that such exploration leads into virtually every aspect of a country's life — economic, political, geographical, historical.

Another purpose for grouping may be to attain needed skills not developed in other ways. When children live in a fluid, exciting learning environment where eager, purposeful activity is ever present, most acquire many such skills as natural, untaught learnings. However, some needed skills may be missed. When this is noted, by teacher or children, those who need the skills will join a group for the purpose of acquiring them, so that they may more easily go on with what they feel they need and want to do.

• A fourth grade has been working independently and in small groups to find out the various ways animals are useful to man and how man has affected the animals. They have been doing much reading and discussing and thinking, even copying out of books everything that has any relationship to the study, but some of the children are getting bogged down. Judy and Linda come to Miss Jenkins with the problem. Upon questioning the group, Miss Jenkins learns that ten of them are having trouble with notetaking. Although considerable attention was given to notetaking earlier in the year, this group knows they have not mastered the skill to the point of using it effectively.

Miss Jenkins suggests they and any others who wish meet that afternoon to pinpoint their problems. Twelve come to the meeting; specific problems are shared and ideas exchanged. Miss Jenkins gets them to think about their real purpose in taking notes, what they are going to use them for, how they can decide what to take down. After working for twenty minutes, they agree to try out their new understanding the next day and to meet together again on the following day to share progress, to ask further questions, and to check their skills by reading some of their notes to the group.

Groups form, shift membership, and dissolve more or less continuously on the basis of common interest. Sometimes they are instigated by the teacher, but more often in a self-directed classroom they develop spontaneously. Such groups may be for a wide variety of purposes and involve a wide variety of activities. Some of them are:

1. To work together in writing a story that may be presented to the class or taped for other groups to listen to and evaluate.
2. To prepare for the reading of a play of their own or one already written for presentation to their class or another in the school.
3. To preview and evaluate a film for use by a larger group or the entire class.
4. To carry out the various functions necessary to the writing and "publishing" of a class or school newspaper.
5. To decide on significant and challenging questions to pose to a larger group or class for the purpose of stimulating involved discussion dealing with the understanding of main issues in an area of learning.
6. To use a listening post with tapes either teacher, child or group made for any of a variety of purposes.
7. To watch film loops, filmstrips, or film and record combinations also for a variety of self-identified purposes.
8. To solve problems of the moment, as when one or two children say, "We need to discuss this with everybody working on our project" or ". . . with everybody playing baseball at noon" or ". . . with those who want to plan what we need to think about when we write stories for first-graders to read."

Notes

This article was written with encouragement and suggestions from teachers (grades 1 through 8) Mary Crawford, Beaverton; Florence Edwards, David Douglas School District, Portland; Elizabeth Gill, Vancouver, Washington; Carole Lisignoli, Portland; Joseph Rubin, Portland; Lynn Rystogi, Portland; Donna Sposito, Portland.

1. Jean Lee Latham, *Carry On, Mr. Bowditch* (Boston: Houghton Mifflin, 1955).

III

Individualized Instruction: Instructional Materials

To conceive of individualized instruction in its entirety is an awesome task. To reduce the task to a manageable size, it may be helpful to define individualized instruction as consisting of three components: 1) independent learning materials, 2) individual objectives, and 3) individual pacing. Learning materials in the individualized classroom must differ drastically from materials used in the teacher-directed classroom. Traditionally, materials, such as texts and workbooks, have been designed to be interpreted to students and not used by them independently. These materials have served and still serve well in the teacher-directed classroom, because interpreting to students is the common practice for teachers and listening is the common practice for students. Individualized programs require students to spend a considerable portion of their time working independently and, therefore, demand materials that can be used independently by students. Consequently, materials that allow students to learn independently are a necessity in the individualized classroom. Early attempts at individualization and the construction of independent learning materials in America found teachers in Dalton, Massachusetts, and Winnetka, Illinois, developing instructional materials called "contracts." A contract set forth a definite amount of reading, exercises, and written work to be done in a specified amount of time. Individualization, at this point, was merely a matter of pacing students through the same material — material that strongly resembled conventional texts. The failure of these self-paced materials was due, at least partially, to their inability to allow students to learn independently.

Without materials that permit students to learn independently, the other two components of individualized instruction, pacing and objectives, are impossible. Individual pacing and objectives infer a classroom situation where students are working on various topics and activities at the same time. If this is the situation, instruction on various topics is needed in the classroom at the same time. If the teacher is the only resource from which the students can gain instruction, the chaotic classroom situation comes into full vision — twenty-five, thirty-five, maybe forty students clamoring for help at the same time. With this situation in mind, the need for adequate self-instructional learning materials is apparent.

In this chapter, various types of special materials designed for use in the individualized classroom today are presented. In light of the previous discussion, a meaningful way to read the following selections may be to evaluate each different type of material on the following criteria that constitute the gestalt of individualized instruction: pacing, objectives, and materials.

Philip G. Kapfer

An Instructional Management Strategy for Individualized Learning

A frequent goal of the administrator is to integrate the essential components of instruction — the teacher, the learner, and that which is to be learned. The problem of integrating these components for the purpose of individualizing instruction is the central concern of this paper.

An instructional management strategy developed at Valley High School, Las Vegas, Nevada, is potentially effective for any school whose staff is attempting to individualize instruction, regardless of the type of schedule being used. To be genuinely effective in the school for which it was designed, however, the strategy was developed within the context of the four phases of instruction which have been advocated by innovators such as Bush, Allen, and Trump. These phases include large-group instruction, small-group instruction, laboratory instruction, and independent study.

Educators should cease to be concerned primarily with the technical problems of team teaching and flexible scheduling. Rather, they should get to the heart of the matter — the opportunities to individualize instruction *provided by* these innovations. The reader may or may not feel that the technical problems of team teaching and flexible scheduling have been solved; yet progress has certainly been made toward their solution. Agreement can be reached, how-

---

Philip G. Kapfer, "An Instructional Management Strategy for Individualized Learning," *Phi Delta Kappan* 49 (January 1968):260-263.

ever, that the problems of individualizing instruction have *not* been solved.

One key to providing for individualized instruction is the preparation of individualized learning units or packages. Such learning packages are the major elements of the instructional management strategy proposed here, and will be discussed following presentation of the strategy.

Assumptions

If a strategy for individualizing instruction is to be effective, it should begin with the currently existing program as perceived by teachers and pupils. In devising the strategy used at Valley High School, several assumptions were made concerning the perceptions of teachers and pupils, and concerning the schedule.

The first assumption, that *the pupil's responsibility is to learn and the teacher's responsibility is to make available to the pupil that which is to be learned*, places responsibility for the teaching-learning process where it belongs. The teacher does not cover a course, but rather uncovers it; he does not need to cover — or talk about — everything that is to be learned by the pupil.

A second assumption concerns the individuality of the pupil. *The subject matter of a course must be appropriate to the learner* with reference to 1) the pace of instruction, 2) the level of difficulty of the instructional material, 3) the relevance of the instructional material to reality as perceived by the pupil, 4) the pupil's level of interest, and 5) the individual learning style of the pupil.

Both the common and the individualized experiences of the pupil result from a third assumption which is related to the schedule: *The size of a group, the composition of a group, and the time allotted to a group should be appropriate to the purposes of the group.* The common experiences which every pupil in a given course should have are primarily a function of large-group instruction. Pupil-centered discussion of large-group presentations may occur in scheduled small-group instruction. Individualized, self-paced, quantity-and quality-monitored learning (that is, the use of learning packages with built-in self-correcting mechanisms) may occur in the laboratory phase of the course. In addition, the laboratory phase should include opportunities for student interaction and should provide directly for the independent study phase of the individualized instructional program.

A fourth assumption of the instructional management strategy is that *before truly individualized instruction can become a reality, learning packages are needed which will provide for self-paced rather than group-paced instruction.*

The Strategy

The instructional management strategy is based on, but does not adhere strictly to, the principles of Program Evaluation and Review Techniques (PERT). In a PERT network diagram, an *activity* is a time-consuming element of a project which is represented on a network as a line between two *events*.

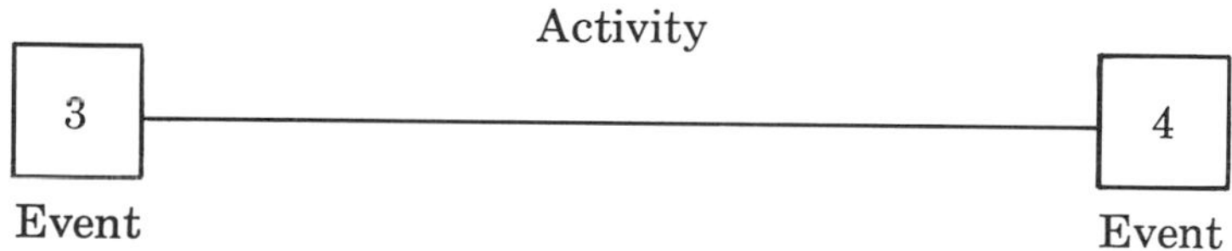

An event is a specific, definable accomplishment in the project plan, which is recognizable as a particular point in time when activities start and/or finish. An activity cannot be started until the event preceding it has been accomplished. A succeeding event cannot be accomplished until all activities preceding it are complete.[1]

The strategy is presented as a network diagram in Figure 1, p. 112. The network is designed to show a sequence in which the pupil will attain an adequate *background* so that he is able to perceive problems and ask questions. The result of his questioning will be internal generation of a problematic *confrontation.* Through study and research the pupil will achieve *resolution* of the problem which he chose for investigation. Thus the sequence in the network is from achievement of *background* to problem *confrontation* to problem *resolution.*

Recycling, for some pupils and for some instructional objectives, may occur at various stages as indicated by arrows in the network. Thus, although the instructional management strategy may be thought of as a design for concept attainment through discovery or problem solving, it is not restricted to this interpretation. In the discovery interpretation of the strategy, the pupil might not be given a statement of the concept under study; rather, he would discover it for himself. In the presentation interpretation, a state-

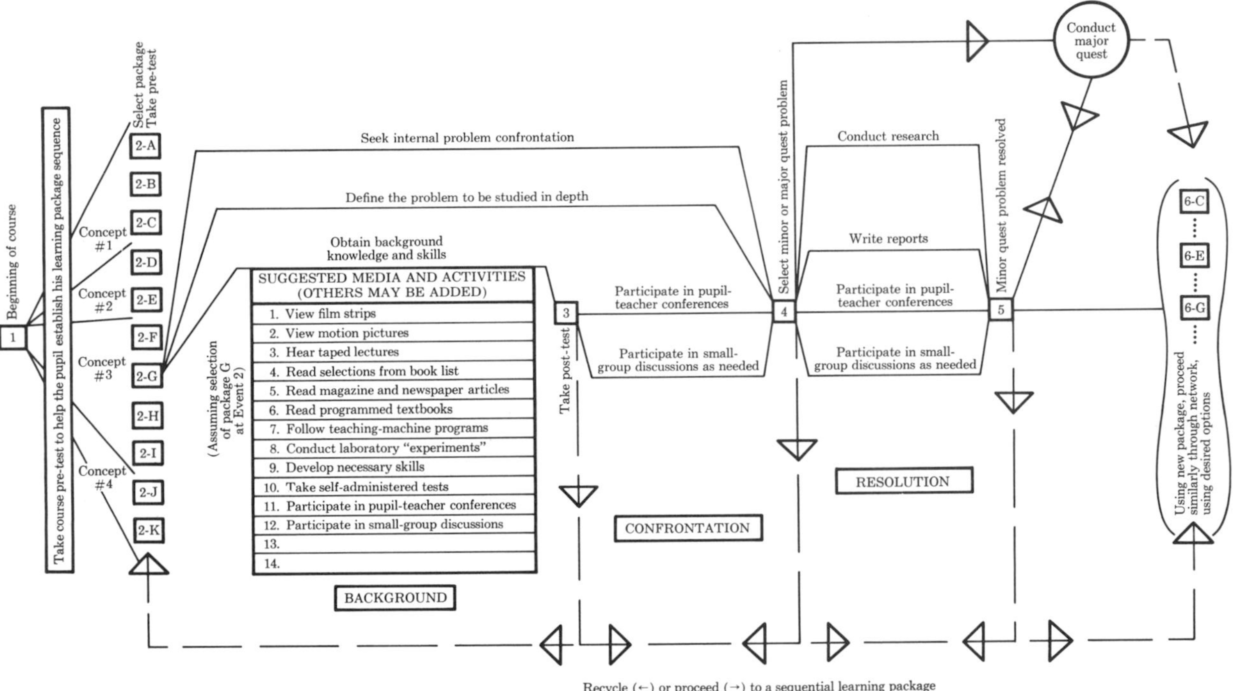

Figure 1. *The Instructional Management Strategy Network Diagram for Self-Paced Learning*

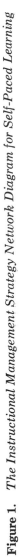

ment of the concept may be given to the pupil at the beginning of the learning package. In either case, the activities and events *following* Event 3 (see Figure 1) represent an inquiry approach. The activities surrounding Events 4 and 5, those involving minor and major quest, give the pupil the opportunity to become a researcher, and in the process of resolving problems the pupil learns information-seeking techniques. When the decision is made to proceed to a sequential learning package, options similar to those just outlined are available to the pupil.

> Change appears in all facets of our society. To facilitate effective and efficient educational change it is imperative that the leaders in our schools assist their teaching staffs 1) to perceive accurately the direction of the change, and 2) to conceptualize a means for obtaining this change.
>
> Mr. Kapfer has developed an instructional management strategy to assist the teachers at Valley High School in doing these two things. The strategy coordinates the direction being taken by the change at Valley High School with a means of obtaining the change. That is, through the development of learning packages, the strategy assists the teacher in structuring a program that will allow each pupil to learn at the pace and depth best suited to his abilities. —
>
> James E. Smith, former principal,
> Valley High School, Las Vegas, Nevada

Preparing Learning Packages

Learning packages usually include the following eight ingredients for individualizing instruction:

1. *Concepts* are abstractions which organize the world of objects, events, processes, structures, or qualities into a smaller number of categories.

2. *Instructional objectives* tell the pupil what he will have to be able to do when he is evaluated, the important conditions under which he will have to perform, and the lower limit or quality of performance expected of him.[2]

3. *Multi-dimensional learning materials* of varying difficulty are cited from commercial sources whenever possible, and include a variety of media which require use of as many different senses as possible.

4. *Diversified learning activities* provide alternative approaches for achieving the instructional objectives, and include such activities as large group and small group instruction, field trips, model building, drama productions, games, laboratory experiments, role playing, pupil-teacher conferences, reflective thinking, and the like.

5. *Pre-evaluation* is designed to assess the extent to which the pupil has already achieved the instructional objectives as a result of his earlier learning experiences. Pre-evaluation enables the pupil to invest his time wisely in areas in which he is weak.

6. *Self-evaluation* is designed to assist the pupil in determining his own progress toward achieving the instructional objectives. Self-evaluation, the results of which indicate the pupil's readiness for post-evaluation, occurs after the pupil has used the multidimensional learning materials and participated in diversified learning activities.

7. *Post-evaluation* is designed to assess the extent to which the pupil has achieved the instructional objectives as a result of his learning experiences.

8. *Quest* includes problem confrontation, delimitation, research, and resolution. Quest is a pupil-initiated and self-directed learning activity.

Integration of the above eight curricular elements in the form of learning packages can serve as an important advancement in providing for self-paced learning through individualized instruction. An experimental course, *Human Relations—an Interdisciplinary Study*, which is currently under way at Valley High School, is based on the instructional management strategy. One of the learning packages developed for the course is reproduced below in the form in which it is available to students. Only the pre- and post-tests have been omitted here due to space limitations.

Learning Package Topic:
Stereotyping[3]

I. Concept Statement

Stereotyping is a learned behavior which results in loss of individuality for members of a stereotyped group or institution.

II. Instructional Objectives

A. From his own experiences, the student will be able to define the term "stereotype" and give at least five examples of stereotyping. He will be able to explain how such thinking restricts his effectiveness in human relationships.

B. Given six general headings and related terms, the student will write the response which he freely associates with each term. By looking at himself or at someone he knows, he then will be able to explain the degree of validity of his free association responses.

1. Physical appearance
   a. red hair
   b. blonde
   c. blue-eyed
   d. fat
   e. tall and dark
2. Geographical location
   a. Southerners
   b. Las Vegans
   c. New Englanders
   d. San Franciscoans
   e. Westerners
3. Occupation
   a. doctors
   b. lawyers
   c. truck drivers
   d. musicians
   e. school teachers
4. Age
   a. teen-agers
   b. over 30
   c. over 65
   d. Old Shep
   e. kindergarten
5. Socioeconomic level
   a. hicks
   b. snobs
   c. happy
   d. unhappy
6. Racial, religious, and ethnic groups
   a. Pollacks
   b. Mormons
   c. Irish

III. Learning Materials and Activities*

A. Scan—current news media.

B. View—"Common Fallacies About Group Differences," 15-minute 16 mm. film, McGraw-Hill.

C. View—"High Wall," 32-minute 16 mm. film, McGraw-Hill.

D. View—"None So Blind," color filmstrip with sound, Anti-Defamation League of B'nai B'rith.

E. Read—Robert P. Heilbroner, "Don't Let Stereotypes Warp Your Judgment," Anti-Defamation League of B'nai B'rith (pamphlet).

F. Read—Raymond W. Mack and Troy S. Duster, "Patterns of Minority Relations," Anti-Defamation League of B'nai B'rith (pamphlet).

G. Read—Earl Raab and Seymour Lipset, "Prejudice and Society," Anti-Defamation League of B'nai B'rith (pamphlet).

H. Read—William Van Til, "Prejudiced—How Do People Get That Way?" Anti-Defamation League of B'nai B'rith (pamphlet).

I. Read—Howard J. Ehrlich (ed.), *Theory Into Practice*, special edition, available from Anti-Defamation League of B'nai B'rith.

J. Read—William Peters, "Why Did They Do It?" *Good Housekeeping*, June, 1962.

K. Read—G. M. Morant, *The Significance of Racial Differences.* Paris, France: UNESCO, 1958, 47 pp.

L. Read—Arnold Rose, *The Roots of Prejudice.* Paris, France: UNESCO, 1958, 35 pp.

M. Read—David Westheimer, *My Sweet Charlie.* Garden City, N.Y.: Doubleday, 1965, 255 pp.

IV. Self-Test

A. Define "stereotype" and give at least five examples of stereotyping. Explain how the thinking respresented in each of your examples restricts one's effectiveness in human relations.

---

*The student selects from the suggested learning materials and activities those which he needs in order to achieve the instructional objectives. He is neither restricted to these suggestions nor expected to use all of them.

B. List your free response to each of the following terms: blond, teacher, teen-ager, parent, Mexican, truck driver, farmer, fat, red. Are your responses accurate? Explain.

V. Self-Test Key

Answers on the self-test will vary. After checking your performance with the objectives and discussing your answers with other students, if you still are in doubt about acceptability you should discuss the answers with one of your instructors.

VI. Quest Suggestion

Select a common stereotype and describe the process of generalization by which this stereotype might have developed. Can you find any evidence to support or refute your description?

Summary

The instructional management strategy is designed to assist teachers in establishing stepwise procedures for achieving individualized instruction. The important elements in the strategy are learning packages designed for use by individual pupils. Identification of the important concepts and instructional objectives which are to be taught by means of these packages will permit the establishment of hierarchical schemes around which the curriculum may be organized, K-12 and even higher. The packages may take many forms, but a common characteristic of each is the provision for self-pacing. As a result, the pupil is enabled to progress at his own best rate, thus avoiding the familiar difficulties of group-paced instruction.

Notes

1. *PERT Time Fundamentals.* Las Vegas, Nevada: Edgerton, Germeshausen & Grier, Inc., undated, p. 3.

2. Robert F. Mager, *Preparing Instructional Objectives.* Palo Alto, Calif.: Fearon Publishers, 1962, p. 52.

3. Charles A. Silvestri and Kathleen Harrell, *Human Relations — An Interdisciplinary Study.* Las Vegas, Nev.: Valley High School, 1967, unpaged.

Larry Frase and Phelps Wilkins

Booklets For Individualized Progress

Teachers hold the key to a power of unpredictable proportions and dimensions—the key to human potential. Too few teachers use this key. They conceal the key—the possibility of releasing human potential — by resorting to homogeneous grouping and group pacing; thus preventing the student from experiencing and developing self-responsibility, self-direction, and self-respect.

The BIP math program, when properly implemented and maintained, is one key which teachers can employ to release human potential.

BIPS (Booklets for Individual Progress) are booklets which contain a sequential organization of mathematical concepts. Each concept is developed from one page on which the objective, samples of problems to be dealt with, and assignments are presented to the learner.

There are five segments to the format of each page in a BIP. They are 1) sequence code, 2) objective, 3) trial test, 4) learning activities and resources, and 5) check-up. Each segment is designed with certain purposes and advantages for the learner. The following is a discussion of the five segments and the purposes for which they were designed. See page 121 for a sample page of a BIP.

Larry E. Frase and Phelps Wilkins, "Booklets for Individualized Progress." Condensed from *Booklets for Individual Progress: Math Key to the Future.* Mesa Public Schools, Mesa, Arizona, 1970.

Sequence Code

In the upper right hand corner of each page of a math BIP, is a code (e.g. M-46-4). The *M* stands for math, the *46* indicates the page number of the BIP, and the *4* indicates the level usually associated with the skill or concept located on the particular page.

Objectives

All objectives are stated behaviorally for more effective communication to the student. A behavioral objective informs the child of exactly what is expected of him. Teachers have been negligent in stating objectives so that the learner knows what he should be able to do.

Trial Test

The Trial Test is a diagnostic instrument for the student to use in determining how well he understands the objective. If the student satisfactorily completes the trial test, he progresses directly to the check-up without spending unnecessary effort on a concept he already understands.

Learning Activities and Resources

All available resources, such as texts, independent activities, games, filmstrips, and transparencies which make references to the particular kinds of problems indicated in the objective, are listed in this section. The learner selects, in conjunction with or without the teacher, those materials and activities which he will employ when he attempts to accomplish the objectives.

When, after practicing with various resources and receiving requested instruction, the student feels he has mastered the objective, he then refers to the Check-up.

Check-up

In this section, the book, page number, and problems which constitute the check-up are listed. The check-up is an evaluation. The purpose of the check-up is to provide evidence that the learner has or has not accomplished the objectives listed on that particular BIP page.

For the purpose of clarifying and unifying the previous discussions, let us consider the following example of the process in which a student is involved, and the decisions he makes when operating in the BIP Program.

The first step the child must take, after he has scheduled time for math, is that of reading the "objective" so that he clearly understands what he is expected to achieve. Next, he assesses his degree of competency in correctly completing problems as described in the objective. As determined by the results of the trial test, the child is directed to one of the following avenues: *Avenue 1* If the trial test shows that he is not capable of satisfactorily completing a check-up containing problems of the nature contained in it, he must seek instruction and practice to aid him in achieving the objective. If this is the student's direction, he refers to the "Learning Activities." The student practices with the materials and activities listed and requests instruction from the teacher if necessary to achieve the objective. *Avenue 2* The trial test may indicate that he can satisfactorily complete the tasks described in the objective. In this case, the student skips the "Learning Activities" and refers to the "Check-up" and completes the evaluation listed there.

Regardless of which of the two preceding choices the student makes after reading the objective, he will eventually progress to the "Check-up" and attempt to successfully complete the tasks listed there. After this attempt has been made, the student refers to the respective teacher's edition so that he may check his work.

The student records at the top of his paper the number of items correctly completed over the number of items on the "Check-up." When the paper has been checked and coded, the student evaluates his progress toward the attainment of the objectives so that he knows whether or not he needs more practice and instruction to accomplish the objective. If the student decides he has not accomplished his objectives, he refers again to the "Learning Activities" for practice and to a teacher for instruction.

The student decides whether or not he accomplished the objectives, and then he places his check-up paper in the designated receptacle so that the teacher may examine it and so that a teacher aide may record the student's progress on the short-term progress chart. The check-up paper is placed in the "out" tray so that the student may pick it up and place it in his folder for storage and use during parent-teacher conferences.

Finally, the student refers to the bottom of the BIP to see if a Unit Evaluation is required at this time, if so, the student reviews the various objectives he has been involved with since the last Unit Evaluation. The student requests the evaluation from the teacher, and when it is completed, he places it in the designated container so that the teacher aide may check it, and the teacher may examine and evaluate it.

Sample BIP

Addition of Fractions With Common Denominators

Objective

After completing this BIP, I will be able to ADD FRACTIONS WITH COMMON DENOMINATORS AND ONLY TWO ADDENDS as shown by solving correctly most of the problems in the check-up.

Trial Test 87

I must demonstrate my ability to add fractions that have common denominators by solving correctly most of the problems given me which contain items such as the following:

1. $1/3 + 1/3 = n$	2. $4/9 + 1/9 = n$	3. $\begin{array}{r} 3/7 \\ +2/7 \\ \hline \end{array}$	4. $\begin{array}{r} 1/4 \\ +2/4 \\ \hline \end{array}$
5. $2/8 + 1/8 = n$	6. $1/7 + 5/7 = n$		
7. $2/8 + 1/8 = n$	8. $1/9 + 3/9 = n$		

(Answers on BIP 88)

Learning Activity

Books

Arithmetic 4, pp. 296 and 266

Programmed Material

Guided Discovery Unit 2

Film Loop And Filmstrips

Fractions (Film Loop)
Adding Fractions (Filmstrip)
Addition of Fractions (Filmstrip)

Practice Sheets

#Skill Sheet 32
*Skill Sheet 37

Check-up

When you feel you have a satisfactory understanding of the objective, ask a teacher for a check-up.

E. Gene Talbert and Larry E. Frase

Guided Discovery Units

Guided Discovery Units (GDU's) combine a somewhat structured inductive study of a principle and three degrees of guidance in the formation of the generalization. Their purpose is perceived as introductory material with supplementary practice material being drawn from available commercial texts as needed.

The major weakness in individualized programs using commercial texts as the core of instruction lies in their use of material designed to be taught as material for independent learning. Typical textbooks require supplementary teacher guidance in the learning process for most children. Only the very bright ones can be expected to use them with an adequate degree of independence. The GDU is designed to provide the needed supplementary guidance for most children.

An important feature of the GDU's is found in the inductive approach and in the method of forming generalizations. The user is provided needed guidance but is left free to do as much thinking for himself as he can handle efficiently. In forming generalizations, he can choose the amount of guidance he wants and can go to an exercise that provides more if he finds his first choice insufficient. Answers are normally provided so that he can check his own work.

E. Gene Talbert and Larry E. Frase. *Guided Discovery Units.* Unpublished manuscript, 1970.

Ideally, a collection of acceptable generalizations written by other children should be available for him to compare his own with.

Exploratory research in mathematics comparing the use of GDU's with an approach using commercial texts indicates that children using GDU's learn as much in approximately half the time and with far greater independence than those using the commercial texts. It should be emphasized that GDU's have neither been extensively developed nor extensively tried out. Exploratory trials, however, are highly encouraging.

SAMPLE GDU

Objective

The student will, at the end of this GDU, write a rule for using the appropriate form of *lie* and *lay*. The student must be able to give an example of how his rule helps him select the appropriate form.

Penny

Penny must have been the laziest dog in the world. Everytime I found her, she was *lying* (1) on something. One day I *laid* (2) my coat on the floor. Immediately, Penny *lay* (3) down on it. If Mother was out of the room, Penny would *lie* (4) on the couch. If she would *lay* (5) the laundry by the washer, she soon found that Penny had *lain* (6) in it.

Penny's favorite pastime was playing with a bone. One day I *laid* (7) a bone in her dish. When she found the bone *lying* (8) in her dish, she grabbed it and ran across the yard with it in her mouth. *Laying* (9) it on the ground, she ran as fast as she could around the yard and came back to see if it was still where it had been *laid*. (10)

1. Look at the sentence in which you find the fifth (No. 5) underlined word in the story above. What does the word *lay* mean in this sentence?______________________________

2. Look at the sentence in which you find the seventh (No. 7) underlined word in the story above. What does the word *laid* mean in this sentence? ______________________

3. How are the means of *lay* (No. 5) and *laid* (No. 7) similar?

   ____

   How are their meanings different?______________________

   ____

4. Look up the word *lie* in the dictionary. Find and copy a meaning that fits *lie* (No. 4) in the story.______________________

   ____

   ____

5. Look at *lay* (No. 3) in the story. Is its meaning more similar to that of *lie* (No. 4) or to that of *lay* (No. 5)?______________________

6. Look at *lying* (No. 1). Is its meaning more similar to *lie* (No. 4) or *lay* (No. 5)? ______________________

7. Look at *laid* (No. 2) Is its meaning more similar to *lie* (No. 4) or *lay* (No. 5)?______________________

8. Look at *lain* (No. 6) Is its meaning more similar to *lie* (No. 4) or *lay* (No. 5)?______________________

9. Look at *lying* (No. 8). Is its meaning similar to *lie* (No. 4) or *lay* (No. 5)?______________________

10. Look at *laying* (No. 9). Is its meaning more similar to *lie* (No. 4) or *lay* (No. 5)? ______________________

11. Look at laid (No. 10). Is its meaning more similar to lie (No. 4) or *lay* (No. 5)?______________________

12. The underlined words in the story above can be placed into two groups of five words each on the basis of meaning. Find the words similar in meaning to *lie* (No. 4) and write them in List 1. Find the words similar in meaning to *lay* (No. 5) and write them in List 2.

List 1		List 2	
lay	(No. 4)	lie	(No. 5)
______	(No. _)	______	(No. _)
______	(No. _)	______	(No. _)
______	(No. _)	______	(No. _)

13. Look at the words you included in List 2. What are some other words which have a similar meaning?____________________

14. Could these words or forms of them be substituted for the words in List 2 without changing the meaning of the sentences in which they are found?____________________

15. Could the words you listed in the Exercise 13 be used instead of the words in List 1 without changing the meaning of the sentences?____________________

Generalizations

G-1. On the basis of what you have learned in this lesson, write a rule which will help you decide when to use a form of *lie* and when to use a form of *lay*.____________________

____

____

____

G-2. Study Exercises 1, 4, and 13 above. Using what you learned about the meanings of *lie* and *lay*, write a rule which will help you decide whether to use a form of *lie* or a form of *lay*.

____

____

____

G-3. Look at Exercises 13 and 14 above. When a form of *lay* is used, you may substitute a form of____________________ without changing the meaning of the sentence.

Look at Exercise 15 above. When a form of *lie* is used, you may *not* substitute a form of____________________without changing the meaning of the sentence.

Using this knowledge, write a rule which will help you decide whether to use a form of *lie* or a form of *lay*.

____

____

____

Thomas T. Haddock

Individualized Instruction through Student Contracts

The increasing awareness of educators, that each child learns differently and at different rates, has caused changes within education. The shift is from the average child as the center of the instructional program to that of recognizing each student as unique and in need of a curriculum geared to his personal needs. Many kinds of grouping procedures have been used in an attempt to meet this need but none seem to provide the necessary flexibility. Educators are recognizing that perhaps the only way to provide flexibility is to eliminate the lock-step graded structure and substitute a self-directed, individualized form of school organization. Donald H. Parker in his *Schooling for Individual Excellence,* (Thos. Nelson & Sons, 1963, N.Y.) said, "Any part of the tract (school curriculum) should be available to any child when he needs it, regardless of whose room or what grade he may be in when he is ready for those skills."

Most popular press discussions have centered on the need for change in instructional materials, equipment and the use of additional supportive staff, but the most critical change that must take place is, however, in the mind of the teacher. The role of the professional teacher must change from one who dominates the instructional area to one who provides activities that allow learning to take place.

Thomas T. Haddock, "Individualized Instruction Through Student Contracts," *Arizona Teacher* 55 (May 1967): 10, 11 and 28.

The frustrations associated with attempting to provide an individualized program without adequate technological aids have led to an innovative approach by a number of teachers in the Washington Elementary School District in Phoenix.

The innovation is the use of instructional contracts based on properly written objectives. These contracts are the very heart of an individual program.

Robert F. Mager in his *Preparing Instructional Objectives*, (Fearon Pub., 1962, Palo Alto, Calif.), stated three questions that are basic to the program:

> What is it that we must teach?
> How will we know when we have taught it?
> What materials and procedures will work best to teach what we wish to teach?

As soon as the first question can be answered precisely then we can begin constructing a vertical line of skills that a student will acquire as he moves through the elementary school. This concept seems simple but it is the most imposing block in the road to an individualized program. For example, if the answer to the question is—I must teach the skills in the fourth grade arithmetic book—it becomes clear that all youngsters must go through the fourth grade arithmetic book without regard to whether the children have mastered the skills, are not ready for these skills, or are ready to begin working on the skills at this particular level. Using this same example of the fourth grade arithmetic book, we can begin to answer the question if we can determine all the skills being taught at this particular grade level and list them in precise language. Then anyone who reads the list of objectives will have no difficulty in coming to the same conclusions as to what we are going to teach.

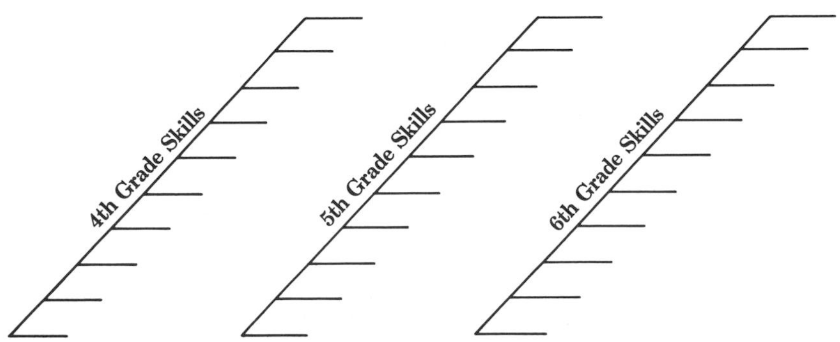

When the precise instructional objectives are identified for a particular grade level, the vertical line of skills can be completed. We can combine this skill development line with the line for the grade below and the line for the grade above providing at least a three-year skill development curriculum.

This is the graded approach and has tended to restrict a youngster to working along this line only within the confines of a particular segment or single grade. To change this to an ungraded, intermediate grade unit takes only a change in thinking and perhaps some movement of instructional materials.

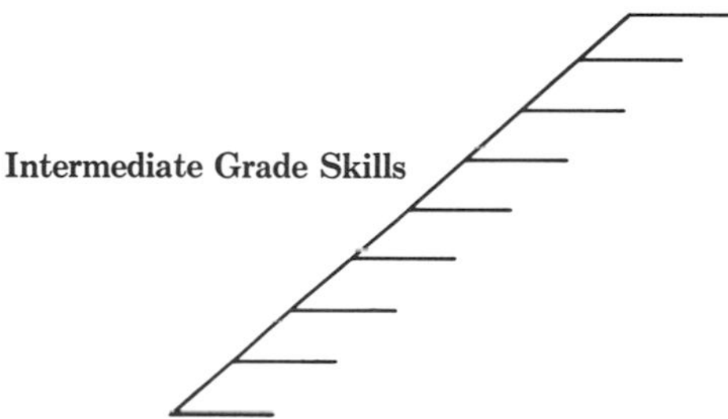

When these grade level expectations are combined to form one continuous line which is available to any student regardless of his room, grade level or his age, the curriculum has been ungraded. At this point we would have an ungraded intermediate unit.

It requires little extension of our thinking to recognize that there will be primary grade children ready to begin working in the intermediate grade unit of skills and that some of the intermediate grade children will be ready for the junior high unit before they have reached that point according to their age or grade level designation. This forces the realization that the educational program must become a continuous progress school including all grade levels or more appropriately, no grade levels with children working along

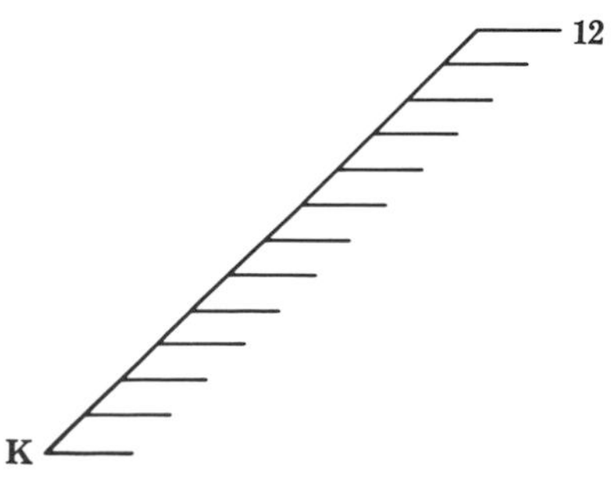

the vertical line at their own particular motivational and ability level.

The second question, "how will we know when we have taught it?" is equally important and one that must be definitely answered in terms that are concise and understandable. It is important that a student be able to correct his own daily work and be tested when he feels ready. When tested he then would be ready to move further on the vertical line of skills or if he failed to meet the criterion he would be given additional work in the area under study, presented through a different media if at all possible.

The third question is, "What instructional materials and procedures will work best to teach what we wish to teach?" This question allows the possibility of providing instructional material of such a diverse nature that the various ways children learn will be considered. The instructional materials should include written material such as would be found in a textbook, skills development kit, resource books, teacher developed folders of materials, programmed texts, newspapers, magazines and audio-visual material which would include the complete range of materials from picture collections to the most sophisticated equipment that is available for the use of the teacher.

It will not appear in the written contract, but the teacher will recognize a need for some children to verbalize and discuss material in small groups and the need for some children to have an opportunity to be physically involved through the use of manipulative materials.

LANGUAGE #051

Name____

Date____

Instructional Objective

Following the instructional program the student should be able to:

Correctly write the singular or plural form of a verb to agree with the subject of a sentence.

Correctly write the plural forms of action verbs.

Criteria of Acceptable Performance

The student should be able to write the correct response with 80% accuracy on an examination based on questions like the following:

The boys (~~builds,~~ build) model airplanes.
He_______________ alone now. (plural of go)

Procedures and Materials Used to Reach Objective Using Good English — Chapter 5, Lessons 2, 3, 4 p. 198-206.

Programmed Text
A-V Materials (see catalogue)

A sample contract developed by Charlene Orth and Jacqueline Moore, sixth grade teachers in the Washington elementary district, Phoenix.

A well written contract provides the answers to the three questions which formed the basis for this approach. The instructional objective clearly states what is being taught in concise language that is understandable to teacher and pupil. The criteria of acceptable performance tells what the student will be doing to indicate that he has learned what he was taught. The steps to the objective provide a variety of sources where the student may find information to help him meet such an objective.

Each student need not work through all of the steps to the objective. Indeed, if he can perform acceptably without completing any of the steps he is welcome to do so. Obvious value is the elimination of review material. Many students do not need this review, and it is a complete waste of time and effort to work through it.

The contracts at first glance may seem to be little more than a new type of workbook but as they are studied more in detail many advantages will appear. One of the most perplexing areas in education is the grading or evaluation of students. Assuming the use of the self-directive, individualized or continuous progress school based upon the use of contracts this area of evaluation may be approached with more definitive information, more objectivity and less opportunity for the teachers' value judgments to become involved with the evaluation process. The students' results on the criteria measures become a record of his achievement as he moves along the vertical skill development line. These results can be interpreted to both student and parents as a report of what he can do and not as a nebulous, unmeaningful grade. The progress of the student will also become obvious as he completes the criterion measure and moves along to the next contract area.

Because this is an individualized project we must recognize that some children will need very brief contracts that can be completed quickly with a minimum of resource hunting while other children will be able to delay their reinforcement of completing a contract over a longer period of time and can be expected to use many of the resources of the school and community.

The use of the contract approach in a self-directive, individualized instructional program should also improve the selection of instructional material. It would no longer be wise to purchase fourth grade textbooks or sixth grade textbooks. Rather, various materials would be purchased based upon the materials needed for the students to reach the instructional goals.

An advantage of the contract approach to education of particular interest to the professional teacher is the obvious fact that the teacher is in complete control of the educational program for the particular group of children with whom he is working. There will be no single textbook, or curriculum guide or administrative edict that will determine what will be used. The instructional materials and procedure will be a professional decision of the teacher based upon the needs and interest of the individual student.

It is exciting to think that teachers can individualize both the rate and way in which children can learn not in the distant future with the aid of a computer but tomorrow in their own classroom.

If teachers in a particular school were to work together in developing and sharing instructional contracts they would have an intermediate or primary unit that is non-graded, self directional and individualized. This also can take place in any self-contained classroom if the teacher is committed to the uniqueness of the individual and is willing to put into practice those things he knows about children and how they learn.

Huber M. Walsh

Learning Resources for Individualizing Instruction

There are several reasons why teachers equipped with proper learning resources can meet individual learning needs in a superior manner. First, instructional materials make it possible for the classroom teacher to "stretch" his time. When resources such as auto-instruction media are utilized to perform certain routine instructional tasks like drill, the teacher is freed for other tasks demanding more creative, human teaching. Second, children *do* have different learning patterns and these necessitate the use of various instructional vehicles to "reach" them successfully. Books and other printed material are the most effective keys to understanding for some pupils, but individual learning patterns may make viewing a motion picture, hearing a tape recording, or working with self-directed programed materials more profitable for others. Most pupils will require all of these and perhaps others in combination. The point is, we have yet to discover a universal skeleton key in teaching children. No single best way to reach all pupils exists; hence, the need is created to find and to use the right material(s) tailored to the particular needs of particular individuals. Third, good instructional materials seem to have built-in child

---

Huber M. Walsh, "Learning Resources for Individualizing Instruction," *Social Education* 31 (May 1967): 413-415.

appeal — a kind of intrinsic glamour and fascination that tends to intrigue youngsters. At least in the beginning, they find most new media attractive and, consequently, are motivated to use them. This phenomenon tends to vitalize social studies instruction and make it more enjoyable. Fourth, certain of the learning resources now available are well suited to individualizing instruction in the fullest sense of the term. That is, these devices can provide instruction on a fully self-directed basis allowing the child to investigate and discover on his own when there is no teacher present to assist him. Innovations in technology have simplified equipment operation to such an extent that pupils can use machines easily. Such refinements have made it possible for children to use motion pictures and filmstrips at home evenings and week-ends as their own private tutors.

Reviewed below are several new resources that hold the promise of being quite useful in "reaching" children of varying abilities in social studies—the slow learner, the culturally-disadvantaged child, the non-verbal youngster, the retarded reader, the gifted learner, and others. An attempt has been made to focus on salient new developments that provide refreshing, innovative approaches to individualized instruction. Most of these are already available to the classroom teacher; others, however, are in the developmental stage and will become available later on.

8mm Cartridge Projector

Because of its compactness, lightness, and simplicity of operation, the 8mm cartridge projector is particularly valuable as a tool for individualizing instruction. It can be used easily by youngsters in the classroom or at home for independent study because the problem of threading film is eliminated. Film is housed entirely within a plastic case and formed into a continuous loop making rewinding unnecessary. Using the projector is as simple as inserting the cartridge, turning a switch, and making minor focus adjustments.

A variety of film loops germane to elementary social studies is available, with most designed to teach a single concept. The ordinary film runs for about four minutes, then repeats itself as many times as desired. This continuous presentation feature makes this a particularly valuable resource in meeting the needs of individuals requiring more than the usual amount of repetition for concept mastery. Such children, on their own, can view and review the film as many times as is necessary to fully grasp the idea. Inasmuch as present-day film loops are without sound tracks, the ideational presentation is exclusively visual, with very slight use being made of printed captions. Thus these films are advantageous for slow readers and pupils with restricted language backgrounds such as those coming from culturally-disadvantaged environments.[1]

The Multi-Media Kit

Multi-media kits are rather complete learning-resource packages containing a wide variety of audio and visual media, printed materials, artifacts, and other learning tools related to various social studies units. They will be particularly welcome in those classrooms where a wide diversity of individual learning needs exist. Each kit contains something beneficial to and usable by almost every child, whether he learns best visually, aurally, or tactually.

The use of kits simplifies the often vexing problem of instructional materials procurement, for it is far simpler for the teacher to procure one package containing an array of media than to have to order each item separately. Its most important contribution, however, is that it provides excellent resources for the individualization of instruction. In a multi-media kit on Mexico, for instance, one would have at hand the following resources: (a) information brochures on Mexico City (these appropriate for use by gifted children); (b) filmstrips with accompanying records (these could be used for research by average children); (c) photographs (slow readers could use these to advantage); (d) a collection of Mexican toys and other artifacts of the culture (non-readers and non-verbal children could make discoveries from studying these articles).

Multi-media kits to be used in cross-cultural studies are commercially available,[2] and, in addition, some school districts have begun to develop their own multi-media kits for social studies teachers.

Programed Materials

The ever-expanding array of programed materials for social studies instruction is an additional resource useful in meeting individual learning needs. Though many of these are intended for total-group use, perhaps their most significant contribution to learning is made when they are used to individualize instruction on a single-pupil basis. Programed materials become particularly valuable for reviewing, reteaching, and re-inforcing knowledge already presented by the classroom teacher. Used in this way programed materials do not supplant human teaching, but instead provide a way to meet special needs of a given learner without necessitating the expenditure of a disproportionate amount of the teacher's time.

One new set of programed materials provides instruction in map and globe skills. This kit, like the two described immediately below, uses very much the same color-coded, sequential approach as is used in the SRA Reading Laboratory Materials. The map program consists of materials to teach basic concepts, study-exercise materials, and self-checking devices.

A recently introduced organizing and reporting skills kit is a program designed to provide instruction in reporting, note-taking, and outlining. Its companion set of materials is a graph and picture skills program intended for the upper-elementary grades. Skills in interpretation and application of graphic materials such as photographs, editorial cartoons, diagrams, charts, and the like are included.[3]

A study skills library will answer the need of many pupils for individualized instruction in social studies reading skills—especially those needing remedial instruction. Comprised of seven different sets of materials, the library encompasses reading levels III through IX. Within each is a series of sequential lessons predicated on a self-directed reading exercise followed by a self-checking activity. Individual lessons are designed to teach such specific skills as interpretation, judging relevancy and significance, verifying accuracy, and finding and organizing ideas.[4]

Automatic Projection Center

A fascinating new idea that is destined to capture the imaginations of creative social studies teachers is the Automatic Projection Center. Capable of a myriad variety of multi-media presentations, the device consists of two sound motion picture projectors (16mm and 8mm), three slide projectors, and a stereophonic tape recorder.

The heart of the center is a punched paper tape that programs the presentations. Equipment is started, paused, stopped, and reversed on command of the tape. Slide projectors may be programed to operate individually, to project in 1-2-3 order across the screen to illustrate a step-by-step process; or all three may be used in concert to produce a cinemascope-like, wide-screen panoramic view. Inclusion of the 8mm projector makes it possible for teachers to augment commercial film presentations with their own inexpensively-made films. The flexibility of tape programing produces almost unlimited possibilities for individualizing instruction. Using the same projection materials, for example, one program can be prepared appropriate to the learning requirements of the gifted learner; another can be made for slow learners; and yet another can be developed for use by average pupils. Though the same instructional media are used in each case, such factors as order of presentation, and provisions for repetition and review are varied according to need differential. Although the APC is not yet commercially marketed, its components and plans for its construction are available.

World Affairs Reports

Teachers searching for resources in current affairs for use with above-average pupils may find what they are looking for in a new series of materials entitled *World Affairs Reports*. Though created for use in secondary classrooms, these materials appear equally well suited to limited, specialized use in the elementary school. A typical set of materials consists of a 25-30 minute sound tape presentation containing on-the-spot recordings of news events as they happened (these made in cooperation with United Press-International); multiple copies of a programed textbook to complement the tape and teach additional information; and a guidebook for the teacher. Kits are to be issued on a monthly basis, and future topics will focus on "The Negro Crisis," "Russia vs. China," and "The Poor." These materials seem particularly well suited for individual use by elementary children as self-tutoring devices. In some cases, however, there may be advantage in using them with small groups of advanced pupils.[6]

Project Discovery

A new departure from customary materials utilization and a noteworthy venture in individualizing instruction is underway at Mercer School in Shaker Heights, Ohio. There pupils take home projectors and films for independent study with much the same ease and regularity that their elementary-school counterparts elsewhere take home their books. This began over three years ago when the school was designated as the pilot unit for Project Discovery—a cooperative effort by manufacturers, school districts, distributors, and universities to investigate the effects of saturating an individual school with audiovisual materials and equipment. An important aspect of the total concept is to facilitate pupil investigation and discovery by expanding the scope of research tools available to the child for independent use.

Each classroom is equipped with both an automatic motion picture projector and an automatic filmstrip projector. Pupils begin to learn to operate these in the second grade and by grade three all but a few can operate them with facility. Adjacent to the school's 12,000 volume library is the film center in which are housed over 1,000 filmstrips and upwards of 600 motion picture films. All materials are clearly labeled and easily accessible to the child user. The center is outfitted with several projectors and headsets making it possible for several pupils or small groups to study motion pictures simultaneously without disturbing one another. The center is available to children before, during, and after school.

An individual with a topic he wishes to investigate may consult a special card catalog to identify the projection materials germane to his research area. Once materials are located, the pupil may view them either in the film center or in his classroom. He may elect to check out the films and necessary projection equipment (with the assistance of parents) for overnight or over the week-end study at home.

Teachers and pupils are enthusiastic about this effort to reduce the usability gap by facilitating self-directed pupil utilization of audiovisuals. Moreover, teachers appreciate having at hand a basic collection of materials ready for immediate use rather than having to guess at future needs and having to order items months in advance of their use.

In addition to Shaker Heights, the project is currently in operation in other cities across the nation in a variety of socio-economic settings. Quite possibly this effort may herald the coming of learning resource centers to the elementary school. Such centers would represent an expansion of the conventional school library into a ful-fledged instructional materials center providing a total spectrum of printed and non-printed resources immediately available to both pupils and teachers.[7]

Computerized Programming for Individualization

A future possibility more than a present-day actuality is the prospect of using automated data processing to aid teachers in individualizing social studies instruction. For example, given data on what a pupil learned yesterday, on his learning needs for tomorrow, and on his optimum learning pattern, data analysis could be used to identify the most promising learning activities and resources to be used with that particular child. For one, this might indicate an individualized session with some kind of electronic teaching device; for another it might mean a small-group work session with the classroom teacher, or perhaps the beginning of some kind of construction project. For others additional work in textbooks might be prescribed. One type of learning resource would be suggested for the gifted, another for the average, and a different one for the slow reader, and so on, accommodating each according to his special needs.

Study-Print Packages

A review of new learning resources for individualizing instruction would be incomplete without at least brief mention of the new packets of study prints becoming available. The typical set contains a coordinated collection of large, full-color photographs centered about a topic or theme such as "Life in the Heart of the City." Although they are good media to use with all pupils, they are especially appropriate to the needs of the slow learner, the retarded reader, and the non-verbal child. Slow learners, for instance, can use them for independent research, recording on tape the information discovered from carefully studying the content of the pictures.[8]

The innovations described are illustrative of new resources becoming available to individualize instruction in social studies. In the final analysis, however, it is not the addition of more hardware to the classroom that will, in and of itself, effect greater individualization of instruction any more than the addition of more hardware to the kitchen produces gourmet meals. Indeed, the critical factor is not a mechanical but a human one. The key point is *how* these media are put to work in individualizing instruction by the classroom teacher. And so, in a very real sense, the most important single resource in individualizing instruction still is the creative teacher.

Notes

1. For additional information, contact The Technicolor Corporation, 1985 Placentia Avenue, Costa Mesa, California 92627.

2. For further information, contact International Communications Foundation, 870 Monterey Pass Road, Monterey Park, California.

3. For additional information on these three programs, contact Science Research Associates, 259 East Erie Street, Chicago, Illinois 60611.

4. For additional information, contact Educational Development Laboratories, Huntington, New York.

5. For additional information, contact Eastman Kodak Company, Rochester, New York 14650.

6. For further information, contact Behavioral Research Laboratories, Ladera Professional Center, Box 577, Palo Alto, California 94302.

7. For further information, contact Encyclopaedia Britannica Films, Inc., 1150 Wilmette Avenue, Wilmette, Illinois 60091.

8. Further information on Study-Print Sets can be obtained from producers such as Silver Burdett Company, Park Ridge, Illinois; and Society for Visual Education, Inc., 1345 Diversey Parkway, Chicago, Illinois 60614.

IV

Does Individualized Instruction Really Work?

E. Gene Talbert

An important question frequently asked is, "Does individualized instruction really work?" From the author's point of view the answer is "Yes." The research evidence is not clear cut at this stage, but an effort will be made in this section to review some of it, draw several tentative conclusions, make recommendations based on these conclusions, and express some of the author's feelings about the problems in individualized instruction at this point in time.

Teacher attitudes toward instructional programs affect their success. A positive attitude by the teacher greatly enhances the probability that students will respond positively to it. A negative attitude almost assures defeat. Instructional materials play a vital role in individualized instruction. Of great concern is the question, "Can all students function well in less teacher-directed programs?" Each of these issues will be discussed.

Rothrock, in 1968, reported a survey of teachers from five western-central states to determine how widely individualized reading was used and how teachers who were using it or had used it felt about the program. Of those who had participated in individualized reading programs, eighty-six percent were continuing to do so although many had made some compromises with more traditional group approaches. Fourteen percent had discontinued the program. It appears, therefore, that teachers who try individualization tend to retain the program or, at least, portions of it.

The theoretical base of individualized instruction was generally supported by the teachers Rothrock surveyed. They found pupil's reaction to be *highly* favorable or at least favorable. It was perceived as fostering self-respect and giving a sense of security to slower learners. It permitted self-pacing and better met the demands of individual differences. Several reported positive effects of individual attention and close pupil-teacher interaction. Some who were no longer using individualized reading programs indicated they intend to return to it at a later date.

Rothrock, also, asked questions about what problems teachers encountered, why they quit using individualized reading, and why they had not used it. The responses are highly consistent with the observations the author has made. Time, class size, inadequate preparation of teachers, and insufficient materials for independent use are recurring themes. The first two are undoubtedly closely tied to the latter two and can probably be subsumed under them. Thus, the crucial problems are inadequate teacher preparation and insufficient materials for independent use.

Teachers' attitudes toward individualized instruction can generally be described as positive. They see it as filling needs in education which they have not been able to meet before. Implementing an individualized program has frequently been difficult. Teachers have begun without first developing adequate skills in diagnosis, prescription, efficient record keeping, and conferencing. Further complications have arisen from teachers having to carry the burden of devising their own materials for the program. It comes as no surprise that much floundering has characterized individualized instruction during the past fifteen years. The first recommendations for improvement of individualized instruction, therefore, are careful preparation of teachers for the programs and increased production of high quality materials especially designed for more independent use.

How can teacher preparation for individualized instruction be improved? Improvement begins with an experience in the approach itself. Increased individualization of classes at the university level provides a model for such a program. Deliberate instruction in teacher techniques of diagnosis, prescription, record keeping, and conducting of conferences can be incorporated in traditional methods courses. The transition to classroom application is eased if student teaching includes experiences in individualized instruction and/or if consultant help is readily available when the teacher initiates the program.

Continuing in-service training is vitally important. Such training should help to integrate the teacher's knowledge of individualized instruction and the on-going or developing program in the school. In the author's experience, many teachers, excited about individualized instruction and proficient in the necessary skills, encounter difficulty integrating their enthusiasm and skills with the school's program. Other teachers, often, do not share and/or understand their feelings and goals. Effective in-service training provides for participation of all teachers affected to achieve better understanding and acceptance of the program and clearer means of articulation within the program.

Increased provision of adequate materials for an effective individualized program presents an enormous problem at this stage. Commercial materials tend to deal excessively with low level cognitive development. Teacher constructed materials tend to be of similar quality. The latter comes as no surprise when it is recognized that the work must usually be done on the teacher's own time with only limited assistance from outside sources.

Many programs now in use rely on published material designed and written to be taught to groups by a trained teacher following a carefully developed teacher's guide. Such material is not appropriate for independent use by students. Wheat found that students often made no effort to read the directions or to understand the examples given in such material. Instead, they asked the teacher or another student how to do the work. Frase reported that students achieved comparable understanding with significantly greater independence when using Guided Discovery Units than when using a program built largely around traditional textbooks. The Guided Discovery Units introduced new concepts and skills in a somewhat structured, inductive approach and encouraged each student to formulate his own generalization with the least possible guidance. Comparable achievement was accomplished in fifty-six percent of the time required in the traditional texts. Programmed materials offer some promise if carefully selected and wisely used. Sartain, in his review of research on individualized readings, suggested a need to combine programmed tutoring with other approaches and to limit it to an optimal duration of approximately fifteen minutes per session. Combined approaches tend to yield better results than programmed tutoring alone.

Academic achievement in individualized programs has not differed dramatically from that of more traditional programs. Sartain reported instances in which individualized reading achieved greater results, achieved inferior results, and achieved results which were not significantly different from those produced by basal group teaching. Weaver and Gibb also reported inconsistent results on the use of programmed materials for mathematics instruction.

Glass and Yager's study of individualized science instruction yielded provocative results. Students who struggled with scientific problems individually or in small groups showed a significantly greater understanding of science as an institution and of scientists as a group than those who encountered the problems and solved them as class groups. Shavelson and Munger found that biology students in a self-paced program demonstrated higher achievement in less class time than those who received group instruction. Eisman carried out a three-year study of the effects of self-paced learning in spelling. He concluded that his evidence indicated learning is most successful when the learner is allowed to proceed at his own rate.

The three studies above suggest some clues to the successful use of individualized instruction. When a process is important, especially higher level ones, such as those required by a scientist, individualized programs which allow the student to experience the same feelings, frustrations, and encounters as those met in the life situation tend to be more effective. Successful individualized programs can be designed which yield comparable achievement results in less time. In skills areas, such as spelling, long term participation in a sound individualized program enhances progress consistent with the individual's ability.

Personality factors and success and satisfaction of students in individualized instructional programs remain somewhat elusive in the research. Independent learning has received quite a bit of attention and probably provides some valuable clues to be tentatively adopted and further studied within the framework of some of the better individualized programs.

Bigelow and Egbert reported no significant differences in personality characteristics, as measured on California Psychological Inventory, between successful independent study students and successful traditional study students. However, within the independent study groups, successful students scored significantly higher on Reponsibility and Intellectual Efficiency than non-successful students. Students were deemed successful if their grades in the course were equal to or higher than their cumulative grade point averages prior to taking the course in which the study was conducted.

Students in the Bigelow-Egbert study were classified as satisfied if they indicated they would like to take another independent study course. These students were characterized as conscientious, dependable, responsible, and concerned about how others reacted to them. Successful but dissatisfied students in the independent study group were more outgoing and sociable than the successful-satisfied students.

Bigelow and Egbert studied university students in an independent study situation. This cannot be equated with individualized instruction in the elementary school as conceived by this writer. However, the findings may provide directions to consider. The need for some caution is sounded by the pattern of response to Sociability items. Elementary school children need peer affiliation. An appropriate individualized program for them includes provision for group activities consistent with their needs. Affective educational goals of self-direction, self-respect, and sense of responsibility — expected outcomes — are evidently related to individualized instruction. Those who possess these characteristics respond very favorably to such a program. It is less certain, but anticipated, that those who participate in a good individualized instructional program will grow in these qualities.

Much research needs to be conducted to determine the affective outcomes of different educational programs. At present, the shortage of valid instruments for measuring affective learning limits the conclusions which can be drawn. It is in this area that individualized instruction holds great theoretical promise. Until adequate assessment means are available, one can only say "Individualized instruction, properly implemented and executed, holds its own in traditional measures of academic achievement and promises more in the development of personal characteristics, such as self-direction, self-respect, and responsibility."

References

Bigelow, Gordon S., and Robert L. Egbert. "Personality Factors and Independent Study." *Journal of Educational Research* 62 (September 1968):37-39.

Eisman, Edward. "Individualizing Spelling: Second Report." *Elementary English* 40 (May 1963):529-530.

Frase, Larry E. *A Comparison of Two Individualized Mathematics Programs on Student Independence, Achievement, Time and Attitude*

Criterion Measures. Unpublished doctoral dissertation, Arizona State University, 1971.

Glass, L. W., and R. E. Yager. "Individualized Instruction as a Spur to Understanding the Scientific Enterprise." *American Biology Teacher* 32 (September 1970):359-361.

Rothrock, D. G. "Teachers Surveyed: A Decade of Individualized Reading." *Elementary English* 45 (October 1968):754-757.

Sartain, H. W. "The Research Base for Individualizing Reading Instruction." Boston: International Reading Association Conference, 1968. Microfiche # (Ed. 024, 553).

Shavelson, R. J., and M. R. Munger. "Individualized Instruction: A Systems Approach. *Journal of Educational Research* 63 (February 1970):263-268.

Weaver, J. F., and E. G. Gibb. "Mathematics in the Elementary School." *Review of Educational Research* 34 (June 1964):273-283.

Wheat, Ronald T. *An Analysis of Difficulties Encountered By Intermediate Studies in Addition of Fractions.* Unpublished honors thesis, Arizona State University, 1970.

Index